A Voice Full of Money

The parable of *The Great Gatsby*
A warning against moral drift

—Study of Scott Fitzgerald, a Voice Full of Dreams

One of the things he remembered most vividly from his days of his early success in New York was that . . . "riding in a taxi one afternoon between very tall buildings under a mauve and rosy sky . . . I began to bawl because I had everything I wanted and knew I would never be so happy again."

For one, eternal morning of desire
Passes to time and earthy afternoon.
SCOTT FITZGERALD

BY ROSS WILSON

"Is there no virtue among us? If there be not, we are in a wretched situation. No theoretical checks, no form of government can render us secure. To suppose that any form of government will secure liberty or happiness without any form of virtue in the people is a chemerical idea"

—**James Madison** (1751-1836), "father of the United States Constitution," fourth president of the United States and a leading advocate of the Bill of Rights. This statement is taken from the debates over the Virginia's ratification of the Constitution.

A Voice Full of Money

The parable of *The Great Gatsby*
A warning against moral drift

Derick Bingham

AMBASSADOR-EMERALD INTERNATIONAL
GREENVILLE, SOUTH CAROLINA • BELFAST, NORTHERN IRELAND

A Voice Full of Money
The parable of *The Great Gatsby*—A warning against moral drift
© 2001 Derick Bingham

ISBN: 1-889893-63-3

Published by:

Ambassador-Emerald International   **Ambassador Productions**
427 Wade Hampton Blvd.   Ardenlee Street
Greenville, SC 29609 USA   Belfast, BT6 8QJ
                                              Northern Ireland

www.emeraldhouse.com

Cover Photo by Snowdon: Camera Press, London.
Used by the kind permission of Lord Snowdon

Cover and internal design by Brad Sherman
Cover design © 2001 Grand Design

Library of Congress Cataloging-in-Publication Data

Bingham, Derick.
    A voice full of money : the parable of "The great Gatsby" : a warning against moral
    drift / Derick Bingham.
        p. cm.
    Includes bibliographical references.
    ISBN 1-889893-63-3 (pbk.)
        1. Fitzgerald, F. Scott (Francis Scott), 1896-1940. Great Gatsby. 2. Didactic
    fiction, American--History and criticism. 3. Moral conditions in literature. 4.
    Ethics in literature.
    I. Title.
    PS3511.I9 G8318 2001
    813'.52--dc21

                                                        2001033819

All excerpts taken from The Great Gatsby are from the Penguin Popular Classics edition.

Penguin Books
Published by the Penguin Group
Penguin Books Ltd., 27 Wrights Lane, London W8 5TZ, England
Penguin Books Ltd., Registered Offices: Harmondsworth, Middlesex, England
First Published 1926
Published in Penguin Popular Classics 1994
15 17 19 20 18 16 14

DEDICATION

To my friend Os Guinness
who longs that the discussion of faith in our civilization
would be as natural as breathing.

CONTENTS

INTRODUCTION

On September 17, 1820, a young man of twenty-five boarded the sailing brig *The Maria Crowther* and sailed down the Thames Estuary in England, around the coast of Kent and towards the Isle of Wight. Thinking of Fanny Brawne, whom he loved and was approaching death, he wrote in a letter on board ship:

"The thought of leaving Miss Brawne is above everything horrible-the sense of darkness coming over me- I eternally see her figure eternally vanishing. Some of the phrases she was in the habit of using during my last nursing at Wentworth Place ring in my ears-Is there another life? Shall I awake and find all this a dream? There must be, we cannot be created for this sort of suffering."

The young man was certainly suffering. He was experiencing hemorrhages and fever, physical collapse, and a breakdown of his personality. When he eventually got to Rome, he was nursed with great tenderness by his friend Joseph Severn in rooms taken at the Piazza di Spagna at the bottom of the Spanish Steps. On February 23, 1821, at four o'clock in the afternoon he called: "Severn! Severn! Lift me up for I am dying. I shall be easy-don't be frightened-thank God it has come." Severn took him in his arms and held him until his last breath. He was buried in the Protestant cemetery in Rome, and as he had requested, the following words were inscribed on his headstone: "Here lies one whose name was writ on water." The young man who died was the greatest Romantic poet in English Literature. His name? John Keats.

One hundred and four years later, a novel was published in the United States of America into a world of post-war euphoria, low unemployment, and a fun-loving generation. It was a very different world to that of John Keats. The combustion engine was transforming everyday life. Henry Ford's Model T was swarming everywhere. By the end of World War I, almost half of the cars in the world were Model T's! This car changed people's lifestyles and the way they thought and enjoyed themselves. As one lady wrote to Henry Ford, "You know Henry, your car lifted us out of the mud. It brought joy into our lives. We loved every rattle in its bones." Here was a freedom which, with the growth of radio, turned the United States into a huge neighborhood. Movement took to the air too, and the aviator Charles Lindberg represented the dynamic spirit of the age. The "American Dream," where anything is possible, was alive and recurring in the conscious imagination of millions. The rich got a lot richer. It was, for many, a world of laughter and endless parties, of jazz and "Flappers," and the dance that stormed America, the Charleston. The god called Hedonism was widely worshipped.

The writer of the newly published novel was a young man of twenty nine years, whose favorite poet was John Keats. That fact deeply influenced what he wrote for he was also a Romantic. He felt deep emotion and cared about where he was and what he was doing when he felt that emotion. The young writer was one of twentieth century America's most gifted writers. His name? F. Scott Fitzgerald. His novel? "The Great Gatsby." The best of Fitzgerald is found in his fiction writing. and nobody could read his novel with any degree of interest and not feel its deep undercurrents of mood and emotion. Fitzgerald spoke of the "hauntedness" of *The Great Gatsby* and he was right, for as Jason Cowley has pointed out, "Lost time and the irretrievability of the past are themes which filter through almost every page of the novel." Some have even suggested that the book should be read like a poem. There is a charm, too, in Fitzgerald's writing. As Raymond Chandler put it, "Charm as Keats would have used it . . . a kind of subdued magic." (To Dale Warren, November 13, 1950, Selected letters of Raymond Chandler, ed. Frank McShane (New York: Columbia University Press, 1981), p. 239).

Fitzgerald and his wife Zelda joined in the exuberant abandon to the hedonism of their day. They participated in its madness and excesses. Fitzgerald dubbed it "The Jazz Age," writing about its rites and passages so intelligently that his work is almost looked on as the actual history of the era. Sadly his lifestyle blighted his life as he attended endless parties from Conneticut to a rented house on Long Island, where months were mainly spent in entertaining or being entertained in an alcoholic haze. He knew the world he was writing about all too well. Inevitably the craze for pleasure became a nightmare.

The novel presents a young man from the Midwest of the United States called Nick Carroway. Nick was working as a bond dealer in New York when he wrote an account of experiences he had centering on a haunting figure who lived next door to him on Long Island called Jay Gatsby. In the creation of the mysterious figure of Gatsby and his world, Fitzgerald found a genre to deal with his deepest feelings. Here can be found the rising tide of moral decadence in his day and the ultimate failure of the "American Dream" to satisfy the needs of the heart and soul. Here is the corruption of values and the decline of spiritual life. The book searchingly investigates how many Americans lost their spiritual purpose as material success wiped out spiritual goals. Daisy Buchanan, whom Jay Gatsby sets his very soul on, has "A voice full of money" but her life is empty of purpose in the midst of her great wealth. Her lament is a memorable one:

"What'll we do with ourselves this afternoon" cried Daisy, "and the day after that, and the next thirty years?" She is a reminder of Marie Antoinette's complaint after her experience with hedonism: "Nothing tastes," she said. Daisy and her husband Tom Buchanan lived in a mansion at fashionable East

Egg on Long Island. The green light on the end of Daisy's dock leads, as the novel unforgettably shows, to only one place: tragedy in "the valley of ashes." It leads to dead dreams and shattered illusions, to meaningless lives, to moral and spiritual emptiness. The wealth of Daisy and Tom Buchanan was wealth, not driven or girded by unselfishness but by an ultimately cruel selfishness where, as Nick Carroway says "Tom and Daisy were careless people. They smashed up things and creatures and then retreated back into their money, vast carelessness, or whatever it was that kept them together, and let other people clean up the mess they had made."

It is, at the beginning of the twenty first century, a thoughtful Bill Gates who has words from the last paragraph of *The Great Gatsby* etched on his portico. It is a very unnerving piece of writing, for there is a hopeful hopelessness about it. "He had come a long way to this blue lawn, and his dream must have seemed so close that he could hardly fail to grasp it. He did not know that it was already behind him, somewhere back in the vast obscurity beyond the city, where the dark fields of the republic rolled on under the night. Gatsby believed in the green light, the orgastic future that year by year recedes before us. It eluded us then, but that's no matter. Tomorrow we will run faster, stretch out our arms farther . . . and one fine morning . . .

So we beat on, boats against the current, borne back ceaselessly into the past."

Is Fitzgerald's conclusion about life the right conclusion? It is worth noting that King Solomon once wrote a book about his search for meaning and satisfaction in life. Probably the best English translation of the title of his book, now contained in the Bible under the title "Ecclesiastes," would be "The Searcher." Possessing huge mental, material, and political resources he wrote of how he built houses; planted vineyards, gardens, and orchards; and constructed water pools. Gatsby also had his huge garden and pool. Solomon acquired male and female servants. Gatsby also hired and fired them. Solomon got himself huge wealth. So did Gatsby. Solomon delighted in music. In Gatsby's life, bands play and Gatsby asks a man called Ewing Klipspringer to play the piano on the day he shows Daisy Buchanan around his mansion. Solomon wrote, "I searched in my heart how to gratify my flesh with wine." There was a colossal drinking of alcohol by Gatsby's guests in his last summer of life, even though he abstained. As for relationships with women, Solomon's sexual appetite was gargantuan.He had "700 wives, princesses, and 300 concubines." What was Solomon's conclusion? "Whatever my eyes desired I did not keep from them, " he wrote. "I did not withhold my heart from any pleasure, for my heart rejoiced in all my labour. And this was my reward from all my labour. Then I looked on all the works that my hands had done and on the labour in which I had toiled, and indeed all was vanity and grasping for the wind. There was no profit under the sun."

So, if that is the summation of what man is able to discern under the sun, that is, in the visible world, is there something beyond the visible world that we can come to know that is not ultimately futile? If the American Dream or any other earthly dream of possibilities and joy is ultimately futile, fleeting, and transient, is it possible to realize worthwhile dreams and lasting joys from another place or source? Certainly. The Christian message emphasizes that Christ declared he had come that we might have life and that we "might have it more abundantly." "I am the living bread which came down from Heaven. If anyone eats of this bread, he will live forever," Christ said. To whom is generally considered to have been an immoral woman that Christ met by the well in a place called Sychar, he said, "Whoever drinks of this water will thirst again, but whoever drinks of the water that I shall give him will never thirst. But the water that I shall give him will

XVIII A VOICE FULL OF MONEY

become in him a fountain of water springing up into everlasting life." "Come to me," He invited, "all you who labour and are heavy laden, and I will give you rest. Take my yoke upon you and learn from me, for I am gentle and lowly in heart, and you will find rest to your souls. For my yoke is easy and my burden is light."

At the beginning of the 21st century, the work of F. Scott Fitzgerald is selling as never before because what he is saying is seen as prophetic in Western society. In this book I have looked at *The Great Gatsby* chapter by chapter, aiming to observe the genius of Fitzgerald's writing and to investigate the moral and ethical themes he raises. I have then endeavoured to relate the positive teaching of the Scriptures as a way out from a voice full of money to a voice full of praise, from a valley of ashes to a mountain of beauty, indeed, to Mount Zion itself (see Hebrews 12: 22-29).

Scott Fitzgerald died of a heart attack on December 20, 1940. He was worn out and aged from the effects of his alcoholism and tuberculosis. All of his novels were out of print when he died. Like Keats, he probably thought his name was "writ in water" and if he did, he was wrong. His writing genius is with us still. He wrote in "The Crack Up" these haunting words:

"The horror has now come like a storm-what if this night prefigured the night after death-what if all thereafter was an eternal quivering on the edge of an abyss, with everything base and vicious in oneself urging one forward and the baseness and viciousness of the world just ahead. No choice, no road, no hope - only the endless repitition of the sordid and semi-tragic"(The Crack – Up, London; Penguin, 1975).

Few writers whom I have ever read have so powerfully described the emptiness of a godless life. *The Great Gatsby* is a warning against moral drift in any society. This book though wishes to state that there is a choice. That choice is to trust

Christ or to reject Him. There is a road. One is broad and leads to destruction, the other leads to life. There is a hope that is "both sure and steadfast and which enters the Presence behind the veil." It is my humble prayer that many through this study of what F. Scott Fitzgerald so masterfully exposes will be led to make the right choice, to travel on the right road, and to know that sure and steadfast hope.

Derick Bingham
Spring 2001

CHAPTER 1

"WHAT DO PEOPLE PLAN?"

There is something in all of us that gets pleasure from being taken into a person's confidence. Nick Carroway has taken millions into his. He is the first person we meet in *The Great Gatsby* and he will, as narrator, be with us until his story is told. But he is more than just a narrator. He makes, against his natural inclination, moral judgements on what he has seen and heard and through his creation, Scott Fitzgerald is telling us what he thinks of what he has seen and heard in the era he named "The Jazz Age." He lived at its heart. Nick is writing from hindsight and has become deeply disillusioned with his experience of living on Long Island in the spring and summer of 1922. He tells his story powerfully, even hauntingly. We must never forget, though, that the narrator is biased because he leans towards Jay Gatsby. His story, though biased, is unforgettable.

Nick tells us that his father once gave him a piece of advice and his received wisdom is a key to his attitude. "When you feel like criticizing anyone," his father had said, "just remember that all the people in this world haven't had the advantages you've had." This advice strangely echoes the famous words of Jesus who said, "To whom much is given, much is expected." With knowledge and advantage comes responsibility and part of that responsibility is not to look down on those who have not got that advantage and knowledge. Nick says he is inclined to "reserve all judgements." This is a Sermon-on-the-Mount value because Christ said, "Judge not that you be not judged."

Nick tells us that this attitude opened him up to all kinds of people sharing their confidences with him because, he writes, "The abnormal mind is quick to detect and attach itself to this quality when it appears in a normal person." This is awesomely true in life. A person who reserves judgement will draw the hurt, the lonely, the abused, the mixed up, and the insecure to pour out their confidences. Jesus, after all, said that he had not come to condemn the world but to save it. The condemned flocked to him, from prostitutes to tax swindlers, from the sick to the discontented rich. People have an unseen antenna for the good listener who reserves judgement.

Of course such tolerance has a limit. Nick Carroway, a Midwesterner, tells us that following the experiences he has had on the east coast of the United States, he wanted no more privileged glimpses into the human heart. He wanted the world to be " in uniform and at a sort of moral attention forever." He admits, though, that Jay Gatsby was an exception to his reaction. Though Gatsby represented everything for which he had "an unaffected scorn," there was something about him that gripped Nick's affection. It was, he stated, his "gift of hope, a romantic readiness such as I had never found in any other person and which is not likely I shall ever find again." What he calls "the foul dust" that floated in the wake of Gatsby's dreams, though, was to sicken Nick. That "foul dust" was, in my opinion, the consequences of sin. No dust is fouler.

The details of Nick's background are given to us in the first chapter of the novel. He graduated from Yale University in 1915. He came from a family of "prominent, well-to-do people" in a Midwestern city "for three generations." He fought in World War I and returned to America restless, feeling he must move to the East and entered the bond business like many around him were doing. In the summer of 1922, he moved to a commuter town on Long Island, instead of finding rooms in New York. For $80 a month, he rented a "weather beaten cardboard bungalow," drove an old "Dodge," and had a Finnish woman who made his bed and cooked for him. Life was "full of promise" and there was "so much fine health to be pulled down out of the young health-giving air." Nick intended to find, by reading books on banking, credit, and investment securities, the "shining secrets that only Midas, Morgan, and Maecenas knew."

Nick's $80 a month bungalow stood "squeezed between two huge places that rented for $12-15,000 a season." The one to the right was "a factual imitation of some Hotel de Ville in Normandy with a spanking new tower on one side under a thin beard of raw ivy, a marble swimming pool, and more than forty acres of lawn and garden. It was Gatsby's mansion." Nick had a partial view of Gatsby's lawn.

Across the bay lay the "white palaces" of fashionable "East Egg" glittering along the water. One evening Nick drove over to have dinner with Daisy Buchanan, his second cousin once removed, and her husband Tom. What unfolds has got to be, in literature, one of the most graphic descriptions of the effect money has on people who are not guided by high moral principle.

Biblical teaching does not despise money for some of the Bible's great characters were wealthy people. We have only to think of Abraham or Joseph of Arimathea. The Bible tells of two very successful business women, one is highlighted in Proverbs chapter 31 and the other is Lydia of Thyatira. Money in the hands of a wise person can be used for great benefit . Faith-based giving, for example, goes far beyond "checkbook charity." Yet the Bible warns that the love of money is the root of all kinds of evil. It can buy medicine but not health. It can buy a house but not a home; companionship but not true friends. It can buy entertainment but not happiness; food but not an appetite. It can buy a bed but not sleep. It can buy a materialistic life but not eternal life.

So it is that on a Long Island afternoon, Nick Carroway is introduced to the artificial, rootless, purposeless, mobile, indifferent, ultimately morally bankrupt and empty world of the Buchanans, the epitome of the hedonistic and wealthy social elite class in the 1920's. First we meet Tom. At twenty one, he was a national hero of American football . We are told that "he had been one of the most powerful ends that ever played football at New Haven," the city in Connecticut which is home to Yale University. He belonged to "an enormously wealthy family" in Chicago. He had come to the East and his greatest recent accomplishment was to have brought a string of polo ponies with him. He and his wife had spent a year in France "for no particular reason" and then "drifted here and there unrestfully wherever people played polo and were rich together." Daisy had told Nick over the telephone that their move to East Egg was permanent but Nick did not believe it, feeling that Tom "would drift on forever seeking, a little wistfully, for the dramatic turbulence of some irrecoverable football game." Tom was 30 with a "hard mouth, a supercilious manner, and arrogant eyes." He had, says Nick, "a cruel body." He is always wanting bigger and better things for his own sake. He has no original thoughts and uses clichés relentlessly in his conversation peppered with his racism.

"I've got a nice place here," he says to Nick, "his eyes flashing about restlessly." Restlessness is the underlining characteristic of his personality and life as it is for a lot of the people Fitzgerald is highlighting. In life, of course, there is no rest in mere possessions. Jesus said that a person's "life does not consist in the abundance of his possessions." Tom Buchanan is a parable of that absolute truth as he turns Nick "around by one arm," moving "a broad flat hand along the front vista; including in its sweep a sunken Italian garden, a half acre of deep, pungent roses, and a snub-nosed motor-boat that bumped the tide offshore." Some people in this world are so poor, all they have is money.

We are, in the first chapter, introduced to Tom's wife Daisy and her friend Jordan Baker. It would be difficult to find a more dreamlike, evocative description of two aimless socialites on a lazy summer's afternoon than this. Of all passages in the novel, this gets etched on the reader's mind for life. "The only completely stationary object in the room was an enormous couch on which two young women were buoyed up as though upon an anchored balloon. They were both in white, and their dresses were rippling and fluttering as if they had just been blown back in after a short flight around the house." Jordan Baker lay motionless and Daisy "made an attempt to rise. Her face was sad and lovely with bright things in it, bright eyes and a bright passionate mouth. There was an excitement though in her voice, which men who had cared for her found difficult to forget. It was a singing compulsion, a whispered 'Listen,' a promise that she had done exciting things recently, and that there were exciting things yet to come." This voice is later described in the novel as a "voice full of money." As for Jordan Baker, Nick writes that "her grey sun-strained eyes looked back at me with polite reciprocal curiosity out of a wan, charming, discontented face."

Of course, with Daisy and Tom, for all their money and social sophistication, there was no high driving moral principle behind their actions, no deep moral purpose to their lives. It is worth reflecting as to whether there is such a moral force and foundation for any of our lives. Was it not the 18th century philosopher David Hume who propounded that we live in an empty, godless universe devoid of purpose? He, along with many other philosophers, thinkers, and writers, including Voltaire, was a Deist. They hold that creation is the creation of the Deity but that this Godhead does not choose or has not chosen in recent recorded history to intervene in His creation. Like a Divine Clockmaker, He has set the machine in motion and now allows it to work on its own accord. God, they teach, has abandoned the earth. Are they right?

Daisy Buchanan's haunting question as she sits down to dinner with her friend Jordan Baker, Tom, and Nick is "What do people plan?" Jordan had suggested that they ought to plan something. Daisy's question is, in truth, at the very heart of the meaning of life. It is obvious in the novel that moral purpose cannot be bought with money. Daisy and Jordan, we are told, engage in talk that has "a bantering inconsequence that was never quite chatter, that was as cool as their white dresses and their impersonal eyes in the absence of all desire." Daisy tells Nick that an hour after her daughter's birth, her hope for her daughter was "that she will be a fool. That's the best thing a girl can be in this world, a beautiful little fool." As Susan Parr has said, "The wish suggests Daisy's recognition of just how powerful intelligence and consciousness can be." Money has led Daisy to deaden her thought process and to let her life drift. Her highest wish is that her daughter become the same.

Tom Buchanan rises from the table to take a telephone call from his mistress and his hypocrisy reeks. By his earlier conversation, he has shown that he is a racist and desires only to selfishly pursue his social position and deny others access to it. Even his reading of a racist's book and his thinking on the subject is an attempt to find something to feed his heart. "Something," says Nick "was making him nibble at the edge of stale ideas as if his sturdy physical egotism no longer nourished his peremptory heart."

From this empty, purposeless, selfish world, Nick drives to his house "confused and a little disgusted." He suddenly finds, as he sits on an abandoned grass mower in his yard trying to gather his thoughts, that fifty yards away his neighbour Jay Gatsby is standing "with his hands in his pockets regarding the silver pepper of the stars." He then notices that Gatsby "stretched out his arms toward the dark water in a curious way and, far as I was from him, I could have sworn he was trembling. Involuntarily, I glanced seaward and distinguished nothing except a single green light, minute and far away, that might have been at the end of a dock. When I looked once more for Gatsby, he had vanished and I was alone again in the unquiet darkness."

The green light on Daisy's dock has become a very famous symbol in American literature. To me it is the call of illicit love, of abandon to "a voice full of money" that has no guiding principle. It leads to disaster. Others will see it as a call to follow one's dreams, "the orgastic future" as the last paragraph of the novel states, which, the novel concludes, eludes us because we are "borne back ceaselessly into the past."

The questions raised by Fitzgerald in the first chapter of his novel are profound and profoundly, the Scriptures speak into those questions. Is life purposeless? Certainly not. "For me to live is Christ and to die is gain," wrote the Apostle Paul. The fruit of the Spirit is love, joy, peace, patience, kindness, goodness, faithfulness, gentleness, and self control. "Against such things there is no law," says Galatians 5:22. Here is profound moral purpose.

As for illict love, the Scriptures do not spare us detail as to where such love leads. It first exhorts that a man love the wife of his youth. "Drink from your own cistern, running water from your own well," it exhorts. "May your fountain be

blessed, and may you rejoice in the wife of your youth. A loving roe, a graceful deer-may her breasts satisfy you always,
may you ever be captivated by her love. Why be captivated,
my son, by an adulteress? Why embrace the bosom of another
man's wife . . . Do not let your heart turn to her ways or stray
into her paths. Many are the victims she has brought down,
her slain are a mighty throng. Her house is a highway to the
grave, leading down to the chambers of death"(see Proverbs
5:15-20; 7:24-27). One would think that one was reading
about Scott Fitzgerald's character Daisy Buchanan centuries
before he wrote about her.

Such truths in Scripture are not written to please some
sect or denomination. They are truths as old as human life
itself, and wise is the person who heeds them. The parable of
The Great Gatsby shows what can happen to those who do
not. When Gatsby had gone in again, Nick found himself
"alone again in the unquiet darkness." Unquiet indeed.

CHAPTER 2

"THE EYES OF DOCTOR T. J. ECKLEBERG"

If the green light at the end of Daisy's dock is a literary icon in American literature, we are in chapter two of the novel introduced to, if anything, an even greater literary icon. We meet the eyes of Doctor T.J. Eckleberg overlooking a valley of ashes.

The valley of ashes lay, Nick tells us, "about half-way between West Egg and New York." It was a desolate stretch of land at the interface of suburbia and the city. It was so desolate that it is described by Nick as "a fantastic farm where ashes grow like wheat into ridges, hills, and grotesque gardens; where ashes take the form of houses, chimneys, and rising smoke, and finally, with a transcendent effort of ash-grey men, who move dimly and are already crumbling through the powdery air." This valley of ashes had a factual basis in that the swamp at Flushing Meadows, in the borough of Queen's, was used as a site for disposal of ashes from domestic heating in New York.

Above this place and "the spasms of bleak dust" which drifted "endlessly over it," the eyes of Doctor T.J. Eckleberg are seen on an advertising hoarding "blue and gigantic, their retinas are one yard high." "Evidently some wild wag of an oculist set them there to fatten his practice in the borough of Queens," comments Nick. The oculist either died or "forgot them and moved away." They now looked out of "no face" but "from a pair of enormous yellow spectacles." The eyes brooded on the valley of ashes, which was bounded by a small polluted river. The train halted there when the draw-bridge was up to let barges through, and passengers could look over the valley for half an hour. The train always stopped there for at least a minute.

Here, right in the heart of the valley of ashes, lives Tom Buchanan's mistress, Myrtle Wilson. She is the wife of George Wilson, a garage owner who is a "blond, spiritless man, anaemic, and faintly handsome." George Wilson calls the eyes of Doctor Eckleberg "the eyes of God." In the novel, those eyes are watching every move made by all in the social class of the elite rich, in the working class of the poor, and in the middle class who commute to work through the valley every day. Fitzgerald is telling us that someone is watching us. He is right, for as Hagar famously said as she walked the road to Egypt long ago, "You are the God who sees" (see Gen. 16:13). He is the judge of all the earth and the one with whom we all have to do. The holiness of God and the holiness He expects does not change in the 1920's anymore than it does in any other decade.

The arrogant Tom takes a reluctant Nick to see Myrtle. They get off the train at the valley of ashes and Nick comments that "the supercilious assumption was that on Sunday afternoon I had nothing better to do." The Christian day of worship and rest is to turn into drunken debauchery before the night is through. The Main Street led to "absolutely nothing," and George Wilson's garage business seemed to be going nowhere, either. Myrtle is going somewhere, though.

In a moment when her husband has gone to get some chairs, she agrees to catch the next train to join Tom at his New York apartment.

The description of Tom Buchanan's steps into the hell-hole of unfaithfulness with Myrtle is measured and powerful. He does not crash his way to the misery of it all but, step by step, its horror is uncovered. Adultery may appear to be as soft as down but before it is finished, it is a raving, flaming vulture.

Myrtle buys a dog from a street vendour on her way to Tom's apartment. It is sophistication she seeks but it is something she will never have. She will never break into the class she is trying to reach even though when she arrives at the apartment, we are told she throws "a regal homecoming glance around the neighbourhood," gathering up her dog and her other purchases "and goes haughtily in."

Fifth Avenue is described as being "warm and soft, almost pastoral on the summer Sunday afternoon." Nick says he "wouldn't have been surprised to see a great flock of white sheep turn the corner." It is not to remain a pastoral scene for Nick for very long. The old hymn that describes the world as being a place "where every prospect pleases and only man is vile" could not put the situation of that Sunday afternoon any better. The apartment they reach is full of "tapestried furniture entirely too large for it, so that to move about was to stumble continually over scenes of ladies swinging in the gardens of Versailles." The hint of the glory of Loius XIV's court is gaudy in this New York apartment, its opulence inappropriate. The whole thing is false and empty and Fitzgerald is exposing it for what it is. Here lies a copy of *Simon called Peter* on a table. While Tom and Myrtle disappear, Nick sits down discreetly in the living room and reads a chapter. It is a hugely potent symbol.

The book was, actually, a best selling novel in 1922 written by Robert Keable, and we know that Fitzgerald considered it immoral. It told the story of a young clergyman who lost his

faith as a result of his experiences in World War I. The theme
of unfaithfulness is being raised here. There are echoes going
back to the story of Christ's disciple Simon Peter, who dis-
owned his Master three times. While Christ was on trial, Peter,
with oaths and curses insisted, "I know not the man." Scripture says, "The Lord turned and looked on Peter" and Peter
"went out and wept bitterly."

Nick is slowly getting drunk as he reads the book and
points out that he has been drunk "just twice in his life." This
particular afternoon is one of them. Betrayal is in the apartment around him and he slowly begins to find that everything
has a "hazy cast over it." Even his attempt to read a chapter of
Simon Called Peter is difficult, for he comments that "either it
was terrible stuff or whiskey distorted things because it didn't
make sense to me."

Together with the copy of *Simon Called Peter* there lies
on the table "several old copies of *Town Tattle* . . . and some of
the small scandal magazines of Broadway." This is not without
significance. Such magazines showed the huge shift in the
cultural climate of the United States. American founders and
framers believed that character held a vital place in the self-
understanding of their civilization. More recent influences do
not. Studies of two popular magazines, *Ladies Home Journal*
and *Good Housekeeping*, show that in the period from 1890-
1910, at least one third of the articles were on character. Yet
suddenly by 1920 the number had collapsed to three percent!
One could guarantee that *Town Tattle* and the scandal magazines had none at all. If a straw shows what way the wind
blows, the literature on the Buchannan apartment table shows
the growing secularity of the era.

Soon a crowd arrives. Myrtle's sister Catherine is "a
worldly girl" of about thirty. Worldly? Fitzgerald does not show
a sympathetic picture of what he describes as worldy. It is shallow. Catherine's hair is a "solid, sticky mob of red hair." Her

complexion is "powdered, milky white." Her eyebrows have been "plucked and then drawn on again at a more rakish angle, but the efforts of nature toward the restoration of the old alignment gave a blurred air to her face." She wears innumerable pottery bracelets that "jingled up and down her arms." She has been to Monte Carlo "last year" with another girl and "hated" the place. Her life is inconsequential and her personality is cold and as brittle as the pottery bracelets she wears.

The McKee's came and are no better. Social climbers, the husband is a professional photographer trying to break into the Long Island set who has photographed his wife fifteen times. The narcissism is blatant, the dullness of his work is revealed in the titles of his photographs: "Old grey horse," "Brooklyn Bridge," "Montauk Point-the gulls," "Montauk Point-the sea."

As the whiskey passes around these morally unattractive people who are getting more and more intoxicated, Myrtle begins to get more assertive and cruel. She denounces her husband who, unknown to her, had "to borrow somebody's best suit to get married in." She says she married him because she thought he was "a gentleman" and knew something about breeding but, she comments haughtily, "he wasn't fit to lick my shoe." Her ugly superiority, her description of the beginning of her affair with Tom Buchanan on a subway train, and her explanation for her unfaithfulness on the principle "you can't live forever" underlined by her "artificial laughter" are a very graphic description of those who live only, as the Bible puts it, "for the flesh." They ignore the fact that life here on earth is short and that the immediate, the tangible, the seen, is not all that there is. C.S. Lewis pointed out that this life is but an inn by the side of the road. Eternity is in everybody's heart, but the Myrtle Wilson's of this world led on by the Tom Buchanan's, live for the present. "Let the devil take tomorrow" is their attitude and he does. In fact, for those who do not repent of such action, he takes all of their tomorrows.

Nick, of course, the narrator of the story, begins to feel the pull of the evil cords around him. He longs to break free. "I wanted to get out and walk eastward towards the park through the soft twilight but each time I tried to go, I became entangled in some wild, strident argument which pulled me back, as if with ropes, into my chair."

The "wild strident" arguments soon got very wild indeed. We read that "some time toward midnight, Tom Buchanan and Mrs. Wilson stood face to face discussing, in impassioned voices, whether Mrs. Wilson had any right to mention Daisy's name."

"Daisy! Daisy! Daisy!" shouted Mrs Wilson. "I'll say it whenever I want to! Daisy! Dai-" Making a short deft movement, Tom Buchanan broke her nose with his open hand. Pandemonium reigns amid "a long broken wail of pain" from "the despairing figure on the couch." There are bloody towels upon the bathroom floor, and "women's voices scolding" as the drunken Myrtle is trying to spread "a copy of Town Tattle over the tapestry scenes of Versailles." From the whole sinful, tasteless, cruel, selfish, aimless scene, Nick and McKee withdraw to a drunken, far from civilized close to their evening. Nick eventually found himself "lying half asleep in the cold lower level of the Pennsylvania Station, staring at the morning Tribune and waiting for the four o'clock train."

Fitzgerald has shown us another side to the seemingly carefree, breaking "Jazz Age." Here is the violent and seedy side. Fitzgerald may not have agreed with Prohibition but he, a heavy drinker himself, is not afraid to show the bad results from excessive drinking. The book of Proverbs gets it exactly right when it states that "Wine is a mocker, strong drink is a brawler, and whoever is led astray by it is not wise."

As Jane Austen, the novelist, was able to put into a conversation between two people in a small carriage travelling in a small area of rural England a microcosm of Georgian England, so Fitzgerald puts a microcosm of the dark side of the United States in the 1920's into a small apartment on Fifth Avenue, New York on a Sunday afternoon and evening in 1922.

Centuries before the post-war boom of the United States, the Apostle Paul wrote a letter to Christians living in the city of Ephesus, a city steeped in all kinds of orgies. "You should," he wrote, "longer walk as the rest of the Gentiles walk, in the futility of their mind, having their understanding darkened, being alienated from the life of God, because of the ignorance that is in them, because of the blindness of their heart: who, being past feeling, have given themselves over to lewdness, to work all uncleanness with greediness. But you have not so learned Christ, if indeed you have heard Him and have been taught by Him as the truth is in Jesus: that you put off concerning your former conduct, the old man which grows corrupt according to the deceitful lusts and be renewed in the spirit of your mind and that you put on the new man which was created according to God in true righteousness and holiness."

Is such a life possible? Through personal faith in Christ it certainly is possible. One thing is certain. It most certainly beats the life Fitzgerald was exposing. He shows us that it was a pit darker and deeper than a lot of people realized.

CHAPTER 3

"WASTING THE MOST POIGNANT MOMENTS OF NIGHT AND LIFE"

The element of mystery by which Scott Fitzgerald introduces us to Jay Gatsby is used very skillfully. We have already seen him in the grounds of his mansion. Nick has told us that he is a man with "an extraordinary gift of hope," with a "romantic readiness" such as he had not known in another person. Jordan Baker has told Nick that she knows the man. At the notorious party at Tom Buchanan's apartment, Catherine Wilson speaks to Nick of being at West Egg "about a month ago at a man named Gatsby's . . . they say he is a nephew or a cousin of Kaiser Wilhelm's." Now we are to meet him face to face. First, though, we learn of Gatsby's parties. The suspense is palpable.

"Every Friday," writes Nick, "five crates of oranges and lemons arrived from a fruiterer in New York. Every Monday, these same oranges and lemons left his back door in a pyramid of pulpless halves." Gatsby's Rolls Royce buses people to and from the city, his station wagon "scampered like a brisk yellow bug" to meet all the trains. On Monday's, "eight servants, including an extra gardener, toiled all day with mops, scrubbing brushes, hammers, and garden-shears,to repair the ravages from the night before."

Once every two weeks caterers set up, with canvas, coloured lights, and buffet tables, a veritable feast on Gatsby's lawn. A bar is set up in Gatsby's main hall "stocked with gins and liquor," prohibition or not. A full-blown orchestra arrives while cars from New York are parked five deep "in the drive." These crowds just arrive and somehow they end up "at Gatsby's door." There is laughter but it is, writes Nick, "spilled with prodigality." The word is chosen carefully. It is corrupt, debauched, wanton, unprincipled laughter. There are introductions but they are "forgotten on the spot." There are "enthusiastic meetings" but between women "who never knew each other's names." There is dancing and champagne "served in glasses bigger than finger bowls." Supper is served twice, the second supper coming after midnight. Even the moon, we are told, is "produced like the supper, no doubt, out of a caterer's basket." Reality itself seems far removed from the world of Jay Gatsby and his parties with their "yellow cocktail music."

One is walking through a modern day "Vanity Fair" at Gatsby's place. John Bunyan had it all filed years ago.We are informed that once people were introduced to these parties, they "then conducted themselves according to the rules of an amusement park."

Deftly, then, Fitzgerald shows us that this world of hedonism is very shallow. When Nick goes by invitation to one of these parties for the first time, he links up with Jordan Baker who is greeted by two girls in "twin yellow dresses." They meet up with them again in a few minutes at a table with three men called Mumble. One of the girls informs everyone that somebody had told her that they thought "Gatsby had killed a man once."

In this crowd, it would not have mattered what Gatsby had done because they are out for themselves. One of the girls named Lucille says, "I like to come. I never care what I do, so I always have a good time." Some of them, of course, never meet their host at all - it matters little.

Nick Carroway had been invited to Gatsby's party when "a chauffeur in a uniform of robin's - egg blue" crossed his lawn with an invitation signed by Gatsby "in a majestic hand." At a laterstage of the party, he finds himself talking at a table with Jordan Baker, to a man about his own age who recognizes him from the war. They talk of France and the war and the stranger recognizes Nick as being from the United States Army's First Division. The man speaks of a hydroplane he has just bought and which he wishes to try out. "Want to go with me, old sport?" asks the stranger. Nick then talks of how "this man Gatsby" had invited him to the party when the stranger says, "I'm Gatsby."

It is Gatsby's smile that wins Nick over. It is a smile that seemed to concentrate on "you with an irrepressible prejudice in your favour. It understood you just so far as you wanted to be understood, believed in you as you would like to believe in yourself, and assured you that it had precisely the impression of you that, at best, you helped to convey." No wonder Nick leans towards Gatsby in all that ensues. In the immediate, Gatsby is called away to a telephone call from Chicago.

A theme is raised in this chapter of Englishness. Gatsby is said to have been "an Oxford man." The books in his library, which is visited on the night by Jordan and Nick, are said by a drunken man who is fingering them, to be real. The high Gothic library is "panelled with carved English oak." Even the "old sport" affectation of Gatsby is a phrase used for the English sense of "being cricket" or fair play. (It is interesting to note that cricket does not have rules, only laws. One would never refer to a sense of fair play as "being soccer" or "being tennis" or "being chess," which are all played by rules). "I've got a man in England who buys me clothes," Gatsby later informs Daisy. "He sends over a selection of things at the beginning of each season, spring and fall." Jordan Baker, who is a professional golfer, later comments that she "was happier on the lawns because I had shoes on from England with rubber nobs on the soles that bit into the soft ground."

The American colonies, of course, had broken with England's paternal hold on them. They had broken away to follow a new dream. That dream is being polluted and Fitzgerald is reconsidering its present state. In this chapter, the phone calls Gatsby takes are from Chicago and Phildelphia. Gatsby "the bootlegger" is being slowly hinted at, later to be revealed as being in tow with the corrupt businessman Wolfheim. The world of Al Capone is not very far away. Jordan Baker, we later learn, leaves "a borrowed car out in the rain with the top down" and "then lied about it." We then learn that at her first big golf tournament there was a row "that nearly reached the newspapers - a suggestion that she had moved her ball from a bad lie in the semi-final round. The thing approached the proportions of a scandal - then died away." Nick states that Jordan Baker "was incurably dishonest. She wasn't able to endure being at a distadvantage." Corruption of values touches all the major characters in this novel, as the seven deadly sins eat into their lifestyles; pride, envy, avarice, lust, gluttony, wrath, and sloth. Even at the party Nick is attending, he is immediately struck by "the number of young Englishmen dotted about; all well dressed, looking a little hungry, and talking in low, earnest voices to solid and prosperous Americans. I was sure that they were selling something; either bonds, insurance, or automobiles. They were at least agonizingly aware of the easy money in the vicinity and convinced that it was theirs for a few words in the right key." Even the "Old World" is being corrupted by the "New World."

The truth is that all kingdoms or empires get corrupted and fall away. The great historian Edward Gibbon defined five basic reasons why the civilization of the Romans, which he so famously chronicled, eventually withered and died. The flaws detected were an undermining of the dignity and sanctity of the home, the spending of public money for free bread and circuses for the populace, a mad craze for pleasure with pastimes becoming every year more exciting and immoral, the building of great armaments although the real enemy was within- the decay of individual responsibility- and finally, the decay of religion where faith faded into mere form, losing touch with life and losing power to guide people.

Gibbon's history includes the first thousand years of Christianity and truthfully shows Christians themselves being corrupted as well as the Romans. It has been strongly asserted that as people read Gibbon's history, it hugely undermined their faith, particularly in England itself in the 18th century. This has had a knock on effect to the present day. Sadly, Christians are as susceptible to corruption as those who have denied the faith. That is why *The Great Gatsby* is, in my opinion, a parable that forces the believer as well as the unbeliever to reassess where they and society stand. The omniscient God is watching us.

All kingdoms have, as Daniel saw, feet of clay (see Daniel chapter 2). The words of Isaiah ring across centuries loud and clear: "For unto us a child is born, unto us a Son is given; and the government will be upon His shoulder. And His name will be called Wonderful, Counselor, Mighty God, Everlasting Father, Prince of Peace. Of the increase of His government and peace, there will be no end." Those who hide in Him will be safe. That fact, though, does not exclude those who do so from the challenge of living holy lives in their communities. Holiness, as the Bible teaches us, is lovely and anything but dull.

Nick's first party at Gatsby's is now moving to its conclusion. A lovely conclusion it is not. "I looked around," says
Nick, "and most of the remaining women were now having
fights with men who were said to be their husbands." One is
hissing "like an angry diamond" into the ear of her husband
who is talking intensely with a young actress. "You promised!"
she hisses. We are told that "the reluctance to go home was not
confined to wayward men." "Whenever he sees that I'm having
a good time, he wants to go home," says one. "Never heard
anything so selfish in my life," says the other. "We're always the
first ones to leave," says the first. "So are we," says the second.
Eventually both wives are "lifted kicking into the night." A
chorus girl is heard first singing, then crying through her mas-
cara. She then "sank into a chair and went off into a deep
vinous sleep."

Jordan and Gatsby have been talking in private for an
hour when Jordan says she has learned something "simply
amazing," asking Nick to phone her later. Gatsby is told,
"Philadelphia wants you on the phone, sir" and with a "Good
night, old sport . . . good night" to Nick, he disappears.

It is two in the morning as a dozen headlights are illumi-
nating "a bizarre and tumultuous scene." A car has had its
wheel shorn off by hitting a "sharp jut of a wall." The collision,
of course, was caused by the error of a drunken driver. His pas-
senger is equally as drunk, insisting that they try backing the
car out even though it was "explained to him that the wheel
and car were no longer joined by any physical bond."

The chapter closes with a lingering sense of loneliness
and waste. As Nick goes to his home from the party, "a sud-
den emptiness seemed to flow now from the windows and the
great doors, endowing with complete isolation the figure of
the host, who stood on the porch, his hand up in a formal
gesture of farewell."

Nick reviews what he has written while he fills in some personal details of his work in New York and his further relationship with Jordan Baker. He makes, though, a comment which perhaps sums up his true feelings of all his experiences: "At the enchanted metropolitan twilight, I sometimes felt a haunting loneliness and also felt it in others - poor young clerks who loitered in front of windows until it was time for a solitary restaurant dinner - young clerks in the dusk, wasting the most poignant moments of night and life." On the wider "Jazz Age" scene, this comment is, perhaps, the most accurate summary of so many lives in that amazing decade in America's history.

CHAPTER 4

"THE PURSUED, THE PURSUING, THE BUSY AND THE TIRED"

It is a Sunday morning and in the villages of Long Island church bells are ringing. They are calling people to worship but there is no response from a crowd who worship in another place - Gatsby's place. Sunday morning finds them "twinkling on his lawn."

Here are the "Old Money" crowd from East Egg. One suspects that Fitzgerald is having a lot of fun with the names he mentions. Here are the Chester Beckers, the Leeches (one can imagine them!), a man named Bunsen (a flame, no doubt), Doctor Webster Civet (cat-like in every move?), and the Willie Voltaires (not to be found in church, for sure!). Here too are "a whole clan named Blackbuck who always gathered in a corner and flipped up their noses like goats at whoever came near."

The "New Money" showing the influence of immigration are from West Egg, including the Poles, the Mulreadys, Cecil Roebuck, Gulick, the State senator, Eckhaust, Clyde Cohen, Don. S. Schwartze (the son), Da Fontano, Arthur Mc Carty, and the Bembergs. There "is a man named Klip-

springer who was there so often and so long that he became
known as "the boarder."

New York was represented by people like the Chromes,
the Backhysoons, the Dennikers, the Kellehers, the Dewars,
the Scullys, and the Smirkes.

Fitzgerald pulls back the curtain a little on the lives and
characters of the people he is writing about. Clarence Endive
"came only once and had a fight in the garden with a bum
named Etty." We learn that Snell was there "three days before
he went to the penitentiary, so drunk out on the gravel drive
that Mrs. Ulysees Swett's automobile ran over his right hand."
The Chrysties, "or rather Hubert Auerbach and Mr. Chrysties'
wife" and Edgar Beaver, "whose hair they say turned cotton-
white one winter afternoon for no good reason at all,"were
there. The young Quinns, "divorced now," young Brewer
,"who had his nose shot off in the war," and Henry L. Pal-
metto, "who killed himself by jumping in front of a subway
train in Times Square," were also present.

At Gatsby's Sunday morning gatherings, people came
from all sorts of corners of society. There was, of course, a State
senator, there were people from the movie business, there were
gamblers and theatrical people like Guz Waize, George Duck-
weed, and Francis Bull. There was a promoter, a tobacco
importer, a man who was once head of the American Legion,
and even a "prince of something."

The question does beg to be asked: Was there a purpose-
ful individual in the whole entourage? If there was, his or her
qualities are not mentioned. Fitzgerald is showing us an America that is slowly changing. No longer do these people gather, as
their forefathers did, around the Scriptures on a Sunday morning as their divinely provided map of the spiritual order. No
longer do they sing in praise to God. It is not the love of God
that is shed abroad in the hearts of these people, but rather the
love of money and the status symbols it can buy. They are wor-

shipping at the shrine of hedonism where pleasure is the chief good. They are far from God's grace, more's the pity. Here is an audacity to transgress, nowadays called permissive but which is in fact trangressive. Its rallying cry is that "it is forbidden to forbid." Here is the forerunner to being as "Bad As I Wanna Be." Whym at Gatsby's on a Sunday morning you will even find James B. ('Rot-Gut') Ferret!

In the fourth chapter of the nove, we get to know the mysterious Jay Gatsby better and the motivation behind his life. Fitzgerald always had a problem with his creation of this character. He first admits in a letter to his managing editor that he didn't know what Gatsby looked like or what he was engaged in, but after careful searching in his model for the character we are about to meet, Meyer Wolfstein, he says he now knows Gatsby better than his own child. Fitzgerald was tempted to let Tom Buchanan dominate the book but, he stated, "Gatsby sticks in my heart" (F.Scott Fitzgerald, "A life of letters" ed by M.J. Bruccoli, Touchstone 1995 page 91). Gatsby's actual source of wealth is never revealed and will always remain mysterious, but it is hinted at from time to time. Wolfstein, who is corrupt, is shown to be deeply involved in Gatsby's business life and Wolfstein is corrupt.

Gatsby now takes Nick Carroway to New York to meet the infamous Wolfstein. At nine o'clock one morning in late July, Gatsby's gorgeous car lurches up Nick's rocky driveway and gives out a burst of melody from its three-noted horn. "Good morning, old sport. You're having lunch with me today and I thought we'd ride up together." Here Fitzgerald captures the spirit of his age in America with deft, brilliant strokes. Thoughtful meditation on his description of Gatsby "balancing himself on the dashboard of his car" reveals his genius in giving the essence of the American character. "He was balancing himself on the dashboard of his car with that resourcefulness of movement that is so peculiarly American - that it comes, I suppose, with the absence of lifting work in youth and, even more, with the formless grace of our nervous, sporadic games," he writes. "This quality was continually breaking through his punctilious manner in the shape of restlessness. He was never quite still, since there was always a tapping foot somewhere or the important opening and closing of a hand."

This author has often noticed this American trait. The United States has an energy that he has never seen anywhere else on earth. There is a "tapping of the foot" or the "opening and closing of the hand" in its people even in the 21st Century. It is a dynamic place. This author once asked a former Attorney General of the United States over dinner what he loved most about his country and he highlighted "Opportunity" as one of its great charactistics. It certainly is a place of opportunity for there is always a restlessness in its people to see what more can be achieved or what new opportunity can be grasped. Americans are usually anxious to get on with it. Is their any other race which is more brilliant at healthily reinventing itself? Sadly, though, for Gatsby his reinvention was partly based on lying.

As Nick is driven in Gatsby's car, in which tragedy will strike, he greatly admires it. "It was a rich cream color, bright with nickel, swollen here and there in its monstrous length with triumphant hat-boxes, supper-boxes, and tool-boxes, and terraced with a labyrinth of wind-shields that mirrored a dozen suns." He found himself "sitting down behind many layers of glass in a sort of green leather conservatory." The United States has, of course, never lost its love for the car. It turned out to be a "disconcerting ride," though, for Nick. As the journey continues, Gatsby begins to tell Nick something about his life saying, "I don't want you to get the wrong idea about me from all those stories you hear."

What Gatsby describes as "God's truth" turns out, in part, not even to be human truth . Gatsby reinvents himself as being "the son of wealthy people in the Middle West - all dead now."

He says he was "educated at Oxford" because all his ancestors had been educated there for many years. By the way, he "hurried" the phrase "educated at Oxford" or "swallowed it or choked on it." Nick suspects he is lying. When he asks him what part of the Middle West he comes from, he replies, "San Francisco." Nick realizes, he is lying because San Francisco is far from the Middle West of the United States. The story that Gatsby weaves is part fiction but the romance of the fiction is breathtaking! He says he came into "a good deal of money" and "after that I lived like a young rajah in all the capitals of Europe - Paris, Venice, Rome-collecting jewels, chiefly rubies, hunting big game, painting a little, all for myself only and trying to forget something very sad that had happened to me long ago."

Then comes stories of the war, promotion to army major, and how "every Allied government gave me a decoration, even little Montenegro." Reaching into his pocket, he produced a "piece of metal slung on a ribbon" and put it in Nick's palm. "That's the one from Montenegro," he said. He even produced a photograph of his Oxford days "taken in Trinity quad." All this, he said, was to "forget the sad thing that happened to me." He indicated that the "sad thing" would be revealed to him over tea that afternoon by Jordan Baker.

On the way to New York, Gatsby is stopped by a policeman for speeding. He waves him away with a white card, explaining that he did the police commissioner a favour once and that he "sends me a Christmas card every year." Mr. Gatsby's ways are obviously not all law abiding ways.

Soon Nick meets Meyer Wolfsheim over lunch. There is wolf in his name and wolf in his nature. Everything about him is sleazy. His conversation is particularly about the night they shot Rosy Rosenthal at four o'clock in the morning. Wolfsheim was there. His eyes "roved very slowly all around the room." He even inspected the people behind Nick's table. Wolsheim is nervous for he has enemies.

"This is a nice restaurant here," he said, looking at the Presbyterian nymphs on the ceiling, "but I like across the street better." The imagery is deliberate!

Wolfsheim's cufflinks are the "finest specimens of human molars." He would have one's very eye teeth for sure! When he leaves, Gatsby informs Nick that "he's a gambler. He's the man who fixed the World Series back in 1919." The corruption of the "American Dream" has now touched even America's sport and the hand behind it sits with Nick at lunch. The shocked Nick Carraway comments, "It never occurred to me that one man could start to play with the faith of fifty million people." Lots of things are "playing with the faith" of the American people in the 1920's and Fitzgerald is exposing them. When Tom Buchanan appears at the restaurant, Gatsby mysteriously disappears with "a look of embarrassment" on his face.

Later that afternoon, Gatsby's motivation in life is slowly revealed by Jordan Baker over tea in the tea-garden of the Plaza Hotel. She tells Nick what Gatsby had revealed to her at his party. It all began back in Louisville, Kentucky, when Daisy Buchanan was eighteen. She and Jordan became friends in Louisville. One day Jordan saw Daisy sitting in a "white roadster" with a young lieutenant from nearby Camp Taylor. They were obviously in love. Gatsby, the young lieutenant, then left for the war in Europe. In those days, Daisy Buchannan was Daisy Fay and eventually she married a man from New Orleans called Tom Buchanan. It was a huge society wedding and Jordan was a bridesmaid. Half an hour before the "bridal dinner," Jordan found Daisy lying on "her bed as lovely as the June night in her flowered dress - and as drunk as a monkey." She had "a bottle of Santerne in one hand and a letter in the other." She wanted to call the wedding off. Jordan and Mrs. Fay's maid, gave her a cold bath and "some spirits of ammonia," and "put ice on her forehead, and hooked her back into her dress." The next day at five o'clock, she married Tom Buchanan "without so much as a shiver."

When Jordan Baker eventually asked Nick if he knew Gatsby in West Egg, Daisy picked up on it and later told Jordan "in the strangest voice" that it must be the man she used to know. Jordan suddenly realized that Gatsby was the officer in the white roadster back in 1917, four years earlier.

She was right and then suddenly, Gatsby's motivation was revealed in a sentence. "Gatsby," she told Nick, "bought that house so that Daisy would be just across the bay." She continued, "He wants to know if you'll invite Daisy to come, to your house some afternoon and then let him come over!"

As Jordan and Nick walk "under a little bridge," Nick put his arm around her "golden shoulder" and drew her towards him. As she leaned back "jauntily just within the circle" of his arm, the phrase began to beat in his ears: "There are only the pursued, the pursuing, the busy, and the tired." He then kissed her.

This chapter raises all kinds of questions but primarily, it is asking deeply moral questions about the meaning of life. Is life to be summed up in the phrase about the pursued, the pursuing, the busy, and the tired? This chapter began with those Sunday morning revellers pursuing pleasure. Sunday is celebrated with secular love feasts that glorify the sexual life. The chapter continues with the deception of one pursuing the dream of a past romance with Daisy Fay. It memorably shows us the corrupt pursuit of money and power in Meyer Wolfheim, and it ends with Nick pursuing his own relationship with Jordan Baker. The spiritual is forgotten in the world of the physical and material. The truth of putting God and His law at the center of life and the circumference taking care of itself is not in vogue. Fitzgerald is to show that this physical and material world is impermanent and transient.

For the believer who seeks by God's grace to stand back
from the life of moral transgression, there are other words
which stand out like a beacon. In the first Bible's Psalm is found
one of the most wonderful descriptions of the truly happy and
fulfilled person. Here is a man who makes God and His law his
priority. The results across history are plain to be seen. Though
such a person was not to be found at Gatsby's on a Sunday
morning, what that person follows is eternally more permanent
than anything hedonism might promise. The Psalm reads:

> "Blessed is the man who walks not in the counsel of
> the ungodly, nor stands in the path of sinners, nor
> sits in the seat of the scornful: but his delight is in
> the law he meditates day and night. He shall be like
> a tree planted by the rivers of water, that brings forth
> its fruit in its season, whose leaf also shall not
> wither: and whatever he does shall prosper. The
> ungodly are not so, but are like chaff which the wind
> drives away. Therefore the ungodly shall not stand in
> the judgement, nor sinners in the congregation of
> the righteous. For the Lord knows the way of the
> righteous, but the way of the ungodly shall perish."

CHAPTER 5

"AFTER THE FULFILLED DREAM, WHAT?"

The novel reaches its height in the fifth chapter. It was Scott Fitzgerald's favourite chapter and his writing ability soars. Here is some of the best poetic prose in 20th century literature. The chapter could almost be called "Ode to a rainy summer's afternoon." We read that "the rain cooled about half past three to a damp mist through which occasional thin drops swam like dew." The lilac trees are "dripping bare." In pouring rain, Nick's lawn "abounded in small muddy swamps and prehistoric marshes." Visible through the rain spattered window, there is now a "corrugated" surface on the Sound.

Here we have the "sparkling odor of jopuquils" and the "pale gold odor of kiss-me-at-the–gate." Color, as in other parts of the novel, is to the fore. Bedrooms are swathed in "rose and lavender silk," while the dresser was "garnished in dull gold." Shirts "with stripe, scrolls, and plaids in coral, apple-green, lavender, and faint orange" are displayed with monograms of "India blue." Gatsby is dressed in a "white flannel suit, silver shirt, and gold colored tie." Daisy's face is tipped sideways "beneath a three cornered lavender hat."

Light is also prominent. Light from Gatsby's house "made thin elongating glints upon the roadside wires." The only sound was made by the " wind in the trees, which blew the wires and made the lights go off and on again as if the house had winked in the darkness." In the music room, "there was no light except what the gleaming floor bounced in from the hall." There were "twinkle-bells of sunshine" in one of Nick's rooms and Gatsby was "like ancient patron of recurrent light." Daisy's buttons "gleam in the sunlight." "See," says Gatsby of his home, "the whole front of it catches light." He flips on a switch and "the grey windows disappeared as the house glowed full of light." Darkness and shadows weave through this chapter, catching the mood and tone of time and place.The writing has dreamlike images; it is Gatsby's dream come true.

The intensity of the pursuit of the flamboyant Gatsby to capture the rich girl who married someone else now comes to its climax. His is the pursuit of a transgressor. What he did was morally wrong and the repercussions were to be horrendous. The Bible talks of the "pleasures of sin" but adds that they are only "for a season." Gatsby's season was to be only for a matter of weeks.

"I've talked with Miss Baker," Nick tells Gatsby at two o'clock in the morning on his return from seeing Jordan in New York. "I'm going to call Daisy tomorrow and invite her over to tea." "Oh that's all right" says Gatsby carelessly, "I don't want to put you to any trouble." "What day would suit you?" asks Nick. "What day would suit you?" replies Gatsby. "I don't want to put you through any trouble, you see."

This is the moment Gatsby has been planning for five years, yet he covers it up. He has spent thousands of dollars in buying a home for it, his every living moment has been motivated by it, and now he tells Nick it is up to him to arrange the meeting! Sinners can be very subtle as they try to hide their sin under many layers. Immoral seduction may be very sophisticated but, the Bible asks, "Can a man take fire to his bosom and his clothes not be burned? Can one walk on hot coals and his feet not be seared? So is he who goes in to his neighbour's wife; whoever touches her shall not be innocent . . . for jealousy is a husband's fury; therefore he will not spare in the day of vengeance. He will accept no recompence, nor will he be appeased though you give many gifts." Jay Gatsby sows the wind; soon he will reap the whirlwind.

When Nick suggests meeting Daisy the day after tomorrow, Gatsby says he wants Nick's grass cut. He then tries to offer Nick business opportunities as if to balance his blatant interferences in Nick's life. Nick refuses it. The white heat of Gatsby's intensity has sneaked out.

Nick calls Daisy and arranges tea with her. He does not inform her that Gatsby will call when she comes around. On the day agreed, "as the rain pours," Gatsby's man cuts Nick's lawn at two o'clock in the afternoon and a "greenhouse" of flowers arrives from Gatsby's with "innumerable receptacles to contain it."

In the pouring rain, Daisy arrives in a large open car. Nick takes her hand, "wet with glistening drops," and helps her from the car. "Her voice," he notes, "was a wild tonic in the rain." Gatsby, having been in the room earlier to check that all was in place and having made himself scarce, pretends to arrive loudly unannounced. He is "as pale as death." Even Nick's heart is beating at the emotion of the unfolding events. No moral principle of the sacredness of the marriage bond rules this rainy afternoon. For the moment, Nick "pulls the door shut against the increasing rain." No door, though, will close out the coming storm in relationships.

Gatsby, when he meets Daisy, is so nervous that he
upsets a defunct clock on the mantelpiece as he leans back
upon it with his head. He catches it and sets it back in its
place. Time seems to have stopped for Gatsby, too. He is living in a dream. Daisy's voice, so famous for being "full of
money," comes from a throat "full of aching, grieving beauty."

Even in the midst of all the intensity, Gatsby lies. He tells
Nick that he earned the moneyto buy his mansion in "just
three years." "I thought you inherited your money?" Nick asks
him. "I did, old sport, but I lost most of it in the big panic - the
panic of the war."

For a time in the afternoon, Nick leaves Gatsby and
Daisy together and stands in the garden under a "huge black
knotted tree." In a dozen sentences, Fitzgerald writes what
are, surely, among the most poignant sentences capturing
mood, time, and place known to literature.Nick stares at
Gatsby's enormous home "like Kant at his church steeple." It
is a very clever comment. Kant is among the greatest of all
modern philosophers. He used to find that staring at his local
church steeple helped order his thoughts. He tried to say in
his philosophy that by perception and knowledge we invent
our own world, and that the invented world has a reality of its
own. Gatsby's mansion was certainly the result of such thinking, as we shall soon learn.

As Nick stands under the tree, he muses on the story
that the brewer who had built Gatsby's house a decade before
"agreed to pay five years taxes on all the neighbouring cot-
tages if the owners would have roofs thatched with straw."
They refused and Nick concludes that "Americans, while will-
ingand even eager to be serfs, have always been obstinate
about being peasantry." The feudal lords of Europe are gone
and there is no desire to return to their hierarchical society.
There is a class system in America, but it is a class system that
is very different to Europe's.

As Nick watches the house, "a maid began opening the upper windows of his house and appeared momentarily in each. Leaning from the large central bay, she spat meditatively into the garden." Somehow that little touch is a definitive moment in the novel. A lot of what is going on would make anyone spit "meditatively."

Now Gatsby takes Daisy and Nick on a tour of his house. They wander through Marie Antoinette music rooms and Restoration Salons. They go upstairs through period bedrooms and bathrooms with sunken baths. They finally get to Gatsby's apartment with "a bedroom, a bath, and an Adam's study," where they sit down and drink some Chartreuse. Gatsby revalued everything in his house according to the response it drew from Daisy's "well loved eyes." His emotional state, in Daisy's presence, now reaches such a pitch that "he nearly toppled down a flight of stairs." "He had been full of the idea for so long, dreamed it right through to the end, and waited with his teeth set, so to speak, at an inconceivable pitch of intensity. Now, in the reaction, he was running down like an over-wound clock."

Gatsby now opens two bulking patent cabinets and takes out a pile of shirts of linen, silk, and fine flannel." The "soft rich heap" mounts higher and higher on the table. "Daisy bent her head into the shirts and began to cry stormily," saying, "They're such beautiful shirts. It makes me sad because I've never seen such - such beautiful shirts before."

What is it that makes Daisy cry? Is it the display of wealth from one who didn't have it when she loved him first? Is it tears for lost love? Is it tears for love of wealth? Is Daisy moved by how far her former lover has come? Or is it simply, "Oh Jay . . .?" Daisy sobbing into Gatsby's shirts for whatever reason is surely saying that Gatsby is defined by what he has and not by what he is.

As pointed out in Chapter one, Jesus once said an important thing about possessions. He said, "One's life does not consist in the abundance of the things he possesses." Try to tell that to the crowds that flock to Gatsby's house! All around Gatsby are people who care more deeply about possessions than they do about the people who own the possessions. In the 21st century, the same attitude is still widespread across the world. It is a false definition of what life is about. Christ asked, "For what profit is it to a man if he gains the whole world and loses his own soul? Or what will a man give in exchange for his soul?" Not even "that huge place there?" as Daisy cried "pointing" when first introduced to Gatsby's house. The last owner's children had "sold his house with the black wreath still on the door." Soon another funeral will take place in the same house, and the minister will begin looking involuntarily out of the windows for "other cars coming to the funeral." Nick will ask him to wait for half an hour but, as he put it, "It wasn't any use. Nobody came."

Gatsby now chooses something very poignant to discuss with Daisy. "If it wasn't for the mist, we would see your home across the bay," he said. "You always have a green light that burns all night at the end of your dock." Nick's comment is pertinent. "Daisy put her arm through his abruptly, but he seemed absorbed in what he had just said. Possibly, it had occurred to him that the colossal significance of that light had now vanished forever. Compared to the great distance that had separated him from Daisy, it had seemed very near to her, almost touching her. It had seemed as close as a star is to the moon. Now it was a green light on a dock again. His count of enchanted objects had diminished by one."

In letters written at the time, Fitzgerald admitted that his novel was about chasing illusions. He is now showing how disappointing chasing illusions can be. The green light, now that Daisy has come, is just a green light again. Its enchantment has gone. "As I went over to say good-bye," says Nick, "I saw that the expression of bewilderment had come back into Gatsby's face, as though a faint doubt had occurred to him as to the quality of his present happiness. Almost five years! There must have been moments even that afternoon when Daisy tumbled short of his dreams - not through her own fault but because of the colossal vitality of his illusion. It had gone beyond her, beyond everything. He had thrown himself into it with a creative passion, adding to it all the time and decking it out with every bright feature that drifted his way. No amount of fire or freshness can challenge what a man can store up in his ghostly heart."

The question before Gatsby is, now what? The truth is that no woman no matter how beautiful or desirable to a man can ever satisfy the deepest needs of a man's soul and vice versa. Popular love songs have always been about chasing, having, or losing that illusion. Klipspringer, Gatsby's "boarder," is commanded to play the piano. He plays "The Love Nest," a popular love song in 1920. "In the morning, in the evening, ain't we got fun," say the lyrics. But the fun doesn't fully satisfy because this god of love does not deliver. On the very capture of this love, it begins to die. In fact when it is all through, Daisy Buchanan becomes morally responsible for the death of Jay Gatsby.

Around A.D. 65, an old fisherman wrote a letter. The fires of his youth were past and one of the mistakes he made was known to an incalculable number of people. He writes to Christians who are beginning to feel the heat of persecution for their faith in Jesus Christ. Is their faith misplaced? Will it turn out to be an illusion? The old fisherman, the now restored Simon called Peter, writes, "Blessed be the God and Father of our Lord Jesus Christ, who according to His abundant mercy has begotten us again to a living hope through the resurrection of Jesus Christ from the dead, to an inheritance incorruptible, and undefiled, and that does not fade away, reserved in heaven for you" (I Peter 1:3-4). Here is a future much better than the present. Here is an inheritance, which is untainted and unfading, to all who believe on the Lord Jesus Christ. There is no marble without its flaw. There is no flower without its freckle. There is no fruit without its blight. There is no face without its blemish. There is no joy without its taint of regret. There is no heart without its sin. Yet to know God through Jesus Christ is to come into contact with absolute purity. This living God can, on repentance toward Him and faith in His Son, bring forgiveness of sins and introduce the believer to a fellowship that is like drinking from a fountain of unfailing freshness and delight. Christ taught that everyone who drinks from votaries of earth will get thirsty again but whoever drinks of the water that He gives will never thirst, for the water that He gives will be as an artesan spring from within that gushes fountains of endless, untainted, fresh life. It's not, for believers, the illusion of a voice full of money leading to disappointment, but the voice of the Good Shepherd, leading His flock on to better and higher ground.

CHAPTER 6

"A SHORT CUT FROM NOTHING TO NOTHING"

Fitzgerald knows the power of suspense and has deftly and subtly kept us in suspense about Gatsby's past. Now all is revealed. A reporter arrives from New York at Gatsby's house, driven by the tide of rumour about Gatsby that has reached his office. He wants to know if Gatsby has "any statement to give out." Gatsby is news.

We now learn from Nick who Gatsby really was. His real name was James Gatz and he came from North Dakota. His parents were "shiftless and unsuccessful farm people." Their son was a dreamer and in "his imagination, he had never really accepted them as his parents at all." He had a "Platonic conception of himself" and lived, in his imagination, in an ideal world beyond reality. A satiric play upon an incident from the life of Jesus is given by Nick in trying to describe Gatsby's *raison d'etre*. After a three days' frantic search, Jesus' parents found him in the temple at Jerusalem talking with the great spiritual leaders of Israel. When his frantic mother asked him, "Son, why have you done this to us? Your father and I have sought you anx-

iously," He answered, "Why did you seek me? Did you not
know that I must be about my Father's business?"

Gatsby was, Nick comments, "A son of God . . . and he
must be about his Father's business." The phrase is saying that
just as God created man and the world, so James Gatz decided to
create a new persona for himself and a new world for that persona to live in. His dream as a seventeen year old became the
father of the man he became. The question is, who is Gatsby's
god? Is it the God who demands a life of holiness available
through faith in Jesus Christ? Certainly not. The god he followed
was of his own invention.

At seventeen he was "beating his way along the south
shore of Lake Superior as a clam-digger, a salmon-fisher, and
in any other capacity that brought him food and bed." It is
well worth highlighting a paragraph where Fitzgerald's genius
captures the imagination created by the flame of youth. What
young person has not felt it? "His heart was in a constant, tur-
bulent riot. The most grotesque and fantastic conceits
haunted him in his bed at night. A universe of ineffable gaudi-
ness spun itself out in his brain while the clock ticked on the
washstand and the moon soaked with wet light his tangled
clothes upon the floor. Each night he added to the pattern of
his fancies until drowsiness closed down upon some vivid
scene with an obvious embrace."

He had attended the "small Lutheran College of St. Olaf's
in southern Minnesota" for only two weeks. This college was
ferociously indifferent "to the drums of his destiny." It was Dan
Cody rather than any other Lutheran ethos that captured
Gatsby's imagination. When Cody's yacht the "Tuolomee"
dropped anchor "over the most insidious flat on Lake Superior," James Gatz was "loafing along the beach that afternoon in
a torn green jersey and a pair of canvas pants." He borrowed a
rowboat and went out to the "Tuolomee" to "inform Cody that a
wind might catch him and break him up in half an hour."

Cody was a very wealthy man, a "product of the Nevada silver fields, of the Yukon, of every rush for metal since seventy-five." When asked his name, Gatz told Cody his name was Jay Gatsby. The reinvention was on its way and for five years, Gatsby was "in turn steward, mate, skipper, secretary, and even jailor. A sober Dan Cody knew what lavish doings a drunk Dan Cody might soon be about, so he provided for such contingencies by reposing more and more trust in Gatsby."

The yacht went three times around the continent when Cody suddenly died. His mistress Ella Kaye made sure Gatsby did not inherit the legacy of $25,000 that Cody left him. Ella got Cody's millions. Cody was a hard, empty faced "debauchee." Sometimes in the course of the parties he attended, "women used to rub champagne into his hair." Gatsby, though, formed "the habit of letting liquor alone." He had probably seen enough of its excesses.

The fascinating attitude of Fitzgerald towards women is raised in the sixth chapter of his novel. It has fuelled much discussion. We are told that James Gatz "knew women early and since they spoiled him, he became contemptuous of them, of young virgins because they were ignorant, of others because they were hysterical about things which in his overwhelming self-absorption he took for granted."

It has been asked, "Are Fitzgerald's women physically attractive but morally unattractive?" They certainly are in this novel. Daisy, for example, is exquisitely beautiful but is flighty. She is implicated before the story is through in three deaths. She is superficial and prone to impulse. Jordan Baker poses like a model. She is intelligent, independent, and articulate but is amoral and dishonest. She is ambiguous. Myrtle Wilson has vitality and an appetite for life. She is sensuous but thoroughly immoral, an immorality about which she is open. Ella Kaye, the newspaper woman, "played Madame de Maintenon" to Cody's weakness and "sent him to sea in a yacht." Madame de Maintenon was the second wife of Loius XIV and influenced his decisions. The women in this novel are restless, highly mercenary, often drunk, extremely argumentative and there is not one who has any real depth. There is no female counterpart to Nick to bring a balanced perspective to things. There is not a truly admirable woman anywhere.

Well might Solomon ask, "Who can find a virtuous wife? For her worth is far above rubies. The heart of her husband safely trusts her; so he will have no lack of gain. She does him good and not evil all the days of his life . . . charm is deceitful and beauty is passing but a woman who fears the Lord, she shall be praised."

So it is a Cody-educated Gatsby who is called on one afternoon by Tom Buchanan, a Mr. Sloane, and an unnamed woman. These three have been out riding and have a drink with him. When the woman invites Gatsby to dinner, they are appalled when he accepts. The question was merely rhetorical. "Old Money" and "New Money" clash once more. It is showing up the rigid class system in the United States of the 1920's, which is a far cry from an egalitarian republic envisaged by the Founding Fathers. The move from Gatz to Gatsby is not, in reality, a move into the world of "Old Money." It never will be. Even Myrtle Wilson, for all her attempts, won't make it either. It is a cruel class system shown by the powerful little cameo of Gatsby going to get ready to follow the three riders in his car, only to find them disappearing under the August foliage "just as Gatsby with hat and light overcoat in hand came out the front door." "Tell him we couldn't wait, will you?" was the excuse left with Nick to pass on to the king of the *nouveaux riche.*

Fitzgerald cleverly links this cameo with a visit of Tom and Daisy to one of Gatsby's parties. Despite Daisy's words, which are always to be taken with a pinch of salt, she did not enjoy the party. She was appalled by it. The evening had a "quality of opressiveness" says Nick and there was "a pervading harshness that hadn't been there before." The novel's duality of attraction and repellence is at work. Daisy is "Old Money" and is appalled that the garish, loud, bold, harsh world of Broadway that came and "begat" West Egg from a Long Island fishing village. Nick comments that these people were being "herded" along "a short cut from nothing to nothing." It is a perfect summary of what they are about.

Gatsby, of course, tries to impress Daisy and Tom by pointing out the famous people who are present. Daisy sarcastically offers Tom her "little gold pencil" to take down any addresses, when his wandering eye takes him off to eat with "some people over there." Now what had once amused Nick turns "septic on the air." Sitting on the steps, Nick waits with the Buchanans as they wait for their limousine to take them home. As a breeze stirs the grey haze of her fur collar, Daisy sings with the music in a "husky, rhythmic whisper." "Her warm human magic" tips out upon the air. Tom, breathing threats of finding out what Gatsby is and does, takes her away. The storm is brewing.

At Belshazzar's party, as recorded in the Bible, the fingers of a man's hand appeared on the plaster of the wall of his palace, telling him that he had been weighed in God's balances and had been found wanting. As this party ends, the results are being weighed and much is found wanting. Disillusion is coming in like grey mist from the sea. Nick and Gatsby talk in the garden when the last lights go out in the guest rooms. Gatsby is utterly depressed because he is convinced, rightly, that Daisy did not have a good time. "I feel far away from her," he says. This is the nearest line Jay Gatsby comes to confessing that he is disillusioned. Fitzgerald once wrote in a letter to Ludlow Fowler about a particular failure that had left him feeling "old." He then made a comment about *The Great Gatsby*. "That's the whole burden of this novel," he wrote, "the loss of those illusions that give such color to the world so that you don't care whether things are true or false as long as they partake of the magical glory" (A Life of Letters, F. Scott Fitzgerald, ed by M.J. Bruccoli, Touchstone 1995, page 78). There is no better summary of the central theme of the novel than this statement. Gatsby's dream was that Daisy would tell Tom that she never loved him. Then when she divorced him, they would go back to Louisville and be married from her house "just as it was five years ago." "And she doesn't understand," Gatsby said. "She used to be able to understand. We'd sit for hours . . ." He broke off and began to walk up and down a desolate path of fruit rinds, discarded favors, and crushed flowers." His dream is fading, the party is over, and the corrupt basis of his wealth about which he did not care as long as it got him his dream has not delivered. His dream is futile. He is faced with Nick's unflinching truth that "You can't repeat the past." He protests and vows that he is going to "fix everything just the way it was before. She'll see." But he is devastatingly wrong.

There comes at the end of chapter six, a description of Gatsby's dreaming that is truly Keatsian. Gatsby describes to Nick a walk Daisy and he had five years before. They were deeply in love and "they came to a place where there were no trees and the sidewalk was white with moonlight." The lights of the houses around them "were humming out into the darkness." "Out of the corner of his eye, Gatsby saw that the blocks of the sidewalks really formed a ladder and mounted to a secret place above the trees - he could climb to it if he climbed alone. Once there, he could suck on the pap of life and gulp down the incomparable milk of wonder."

There is a parallel here to Jacob's ladder but it is worth remembering that in the Bible story God was not at the top of the ladder but was with the dreaming Jacob at the bottom. When Jacob awoke he said, "Surely the Lord is in this place." Bible truth is not illusionary. It is the greatest possible reality.

Knowing God in the experiences of life makes the milk of wonder in life even more wonderful. Chasing illusionary dreams without God is bound to end up in disappointment and disillusion. Jacob's manipulation of people for his own ends had brought him to this place of dreaming with his head upon a stone for a pillow.God's word to him was to be an awesome experience. So it is that in the New Testament, Paul calls the Scriptures, which are God's word to mankind, "the sincere milk of the word." By them, he teaches and people grow. In chasing the milk of wonder he was after, Gatsby never grew but stayed a dreaming seventeen year old.

Gatsby kisses Daisy. Nick is so caught up in his description of his experience that he, for one moment perhaps the only one in the whole story, empathizes with Gatsby. He tries to remember a phrase he had heard in his past that summed up his feeling, but it would not come.

Of the kiss Gatsby had with Daisy, the comment is made that "he knew when he kissed this girl and forever wed his unutterable visions to her perishable breath, his mind would never romp again like the mind of God." What does this imply? It implies that what he is seeking for in his deepest heart is made real for him in a woman whose breath we are told is "perishable." We are again facing the fact that nothing can take the place of God. Nothing. All of us want to gulp down the milk of wonder but one thing is for sure, the Great Gatsby did not find it in Daisy Buchanan. Chasing his dream was a short cut from nowhere to nowhere.

CHAPTER 7

"WATCHING OVER NOTHING"

In a poem called "Prospice," Robert Browning writes of approaching death. He speaks of the time "When the snows begin and the blasts denote I am nearing the place." He writes of "The power of the night, the press of the storm, the post of the foe; where he stands the Arch Fear is in a visible form." Death in *The Great Gatsby* is also treated as a formidable foe and the "Arch Fear" comes on a simmering hot day in New York State amid the full blast of a matrimonial storm. If any of us is ever tempted to think that unfaithfulness in marriage and a libertine lifestyle brings sheer lasting bliss and has no serious, heart-breaking consequences, then F. Scott Fitzgerald will cause us to think again.

In the novel *Anna Karenina*, arguably the greatest novel ever written, Count Tolstoy shows the aftermath of the breaking of a marriage against the huge canvas of Czarist Russia, ending in Anna's suicide. In *The Great Gatsby*, among the foremost of all American novels, Fitzgerald shows the aftermath of unfaithfulness in marriage and moral drift against the canvas of what has been named "The Roaring Twenties" in the United States of America. In the seventh chapter he shows the full blast of the storm gradually, with marked artistic control. The end is every bit as tragic as Anna's.

First, we are shown the death of Gatsby's weekend parties. The whole gaudy spree finishes because Daisy did not approve. "The whole caravansary had fallen in like a card house at the disapproval in her eyes," comments Nick. The church bells in "the villages alongshore" would still ring out on a Sunday morning, but "the world and his mistress" would not "twinkle hilariously" on Gatsby's lawn anymore. Their "twinkle" had dimmed. They would move on somewhere else, as they always do, and would not care less about what they left behind. Fools they are, who try to light their pathway through life by their fires or torches. In the immortal words of Isaiah the prophet, "Let him who walks in the dark, who has no light, trust in the name of the Lord and rely on his God." Isaiah further delivers God's verdict on those who follow their own light. He writes, "But now all who light fires and provide yourselves with flaming torches, go, walk in the light of your fires and of the torches you have set ablaze. This is what you shall receive from my hand; you will lie down in torment."

Nick is to have his eyes opened to what is really going on in Gatsby's world. In the words of Tiresias in the Greek tragedy "Odipus the King" by the great Sopochles, "How terrible - to see the truth when the truth is only pain to him who sees!" The first portent of the coming storm came to him when he noticed that the lights in Gatsby's house failed to go on one Saturday night and he summarizes, "as obscurely as it had begun, his career as Trimalchio was over." Trimalchio was an ostentatious patron and party giver in *Satyricon*, the satirical work by the Roman writer Petronuis. Fitzgerald had considered calling his novel "Trimalchio" or "Trimalchio in West Egg." Time has shown that his final choice was much better, for the title *The Great Gatsby* was a comment on the illusionary dreams of Jimmy Gatz of North Dakota.

Nick went over to Gatsby's house, having further noticed that "the automobiles which turned expectantly into his drive stayed for just a moment and then drove sulkily away." He was greeted by a butler who was unfamiliar and had a "villainous face." When Nick asks if Mr.Gatsby is sick, he is grudgingly told that he is not. On telling the butler to inform Gatsby that Mr.Carroway had called, he finds the door is abruptly slammed behind him. Gatsby's glitter is coming off for certain. Later, Nick learns that Gatsby has dismissed all of his servants and replaced them with half a dozen people sent to him by Meyer Wolfsheim. The wolf is now inside the door and his cold, calculating self interest will soon surface.

Gatsby telephones the next day to invite Nick, at Daisy's request, to come to her house "for lunch tomorrow" with Jordan Baker. The day turns out to be the warmest day of the summer and Fitzgerald's description of its effect on people is masterly. His use of detail is superb. First, he describes his morning ride home on the train out of New York City where "the straw seats of the car hovered on the edge of combustion," and where the woman next to him "perspired delicately into her white shirtwaist." The conductor hands Nick's ticket back "with a dark stain from his hand." There is a clever little aside showing the genius of Fitzgerald's writing where Nick comments, "That anyone should care in this heat whose flushed lips he kissed, or whose head made damp the pajama pocket over his heart." The unromantic nature of the afternoon is put most succinctly!

Nick soon finds himself back at the Buchanan's household where the situation is heating up in more ways than one. Daisy, who kisses Gatsby in Nick and Jordan's presence while Tom is out of the room says, when gently scolded by Jordan, "I don't care!" and begins to "clog on the fireplace." When her little girl comes into the room with her nurse, Gatsby is faced with reality but even then the reality is simply "shown off" in her pretty clothes. "You little dream, you," says Daisy. She is treated as a possession, an "it" rather than being treated as a real living child with a life and space of her own. Her piercing question, "Where's Daddy?" is ignored and after she leaves, Daisy describes her as looking like her mother. Any reality that the child brings to the situation is removed with the nurse's, "Come Pammy." Any truth of the Bible's prophecy that one day on earth "a little child shall lead them" has no place in the Buchanan's world. Soon the idle, careless, purposeless, unprincipled Daisy cries, "What'll we do with ourselves this afternoon and the day after that and the next thirty years?" She suggests that they "go to town" and the looks between herself and Gatsby reveal to Tom that something is going on between them.

As the women get ready, Gatsby informs Nick that he can't say anything in Tom's house. Nick replies by pointing out that Daisy has "got an indiscreet voice." "It's full of . . . her voice is full of money," says Gatsby suddenly. It is a perfect description. "Old money" circumscribes her lifestyle, her acquaintances, her friends, her movements, her attitudes. It also leaves her life empty and without qualities, as she abdicates responsibility. "I don't care!" is her reply to any questioning of her recklessness. It had a charm, that voice of Daisy's, that voice full of money, for "that was the inexhaustible charm that rose and fell in it, the cymbal's song of it . . . high in a white palace the king's daughter, the golden girl . . . ," Nick writes euphemistically. The reality of its cruelty will soon be known. It is worth repeating the Bible's famous comment: "Charm is deceitful but a woman who fears the Lord, she shall be praised." Daisy Buchanan will illicit no praise from any reader as this story ends.

Eventually they all drive, at Daisy's suggestion, "to town." Tom drives Nick and Jordan in Gatsby's car and Gatsby drives Daisy in Tom's coupé. Tom begins to rail against Gatsby. He deeply questions Gatsby's story. Nick observes that they "Were all irritable now with the fading ale," and being aware of it, they "drove for a while in silence."

Fitzgerald is making a very clear point here about the effect of alcohol on the body. Alcohol, of course, is always depressant and inhibitory. Paradoxically, of course, the effect of small doses appears to bring relaxation, to reduce a sense of stress, to give feelings of pleasure or well-being; but alcohol does that by actually depressing the normal inhibitory systems in the higher centers of the brain. Any feelings of pleasure and well-being are short lived and often it takes more and more to produce the same effect. Alcohol allows the more basic instincts to emerge, as this journey to New York was showing.

Tom stops for gas at George Wilson's and the garage proprietor informs Tom that he and his wife are going away. He insists that his wife is going "whether she wants to or not." Nick notices Myrtle Wilson's face in an upstairs window, "her eyes made wide with jealous terror," and fixed on Jordan Baker whom she took to be Tom's wife. Over the as heaps, the giant eyes of Doctor T. J. Eckleberg still kept their vigil. Soon, tragedy would come into view.

Tom is now aware that his wife and mistress were "slipping precipately from his control." He confronts Gatsby in a "large and stifling room," the parlour of a suite in the Plaza Hotel that they had engaged. The confrontation becomes as heated as the room they temporarily occupy. Below them, a wedding is taking place and the "portentous chords of Mendelssohn's Wedding March" reach them. Tom questions Gatsby's attendance at Oxford University and Gatsby defends his attendance there for five months after the war. Tom then confronts Gatsby about his affair with Daisy and says, "Nowa-

days people begin by sneering at family life and family institu-
tions. Next, they'll throw everything overboard and have
intermarriage with black and white." Nick, now angry, is
tempted to laugh at Tom's talk and observes Nick, "The transi-
tion from libertine to prig was so complete." Tom Buchanan's
hypocrisy is stark.

The argument rages on with Gatsby telling Tom that his
wife never loved him. Daisy admits to this but then retracts
her statement by saying, "Even I alone can't say I never loved
Tom. It wouldn't be true." Daisy, though, backs Gatsby in saying that she is going to leave her husband. Tom, now really
boiling with anger, accuses Gatsby of being "a common
swindler" in league with Meyer Wolfheim, buying up "side-
street day-stores," selling grain alcohol over the counter, and
letting his friend Walter Chase, who was in on the deal, go to
jail for a month. "That drug store business was just small
change," says Tom, adding that he is sure Gatsby has "got
something on now that Walter's afraid to tell me."

Nick describes Gatsby as looking as if he had "killed a
man." We are never, in fact, to know the full detail of all that
went on. Eventually, Daisy pleads to be allowed to go and
then Gatsby and she "were gone," opines Nick, "without a
word, snapped out, made accidental, isolated, like ghosts,
even from our pity."

Nick suddenly realizes it is his thirtieth birthday but as
he heads back with Tom and Jordan Baker to East Egg, he
feels that stretching before him is "the portentous, menacing
road of a new decade." America was soon to experience such a
menacing and lonely road in the coming Great Depression.
Was Scott Fitzgerald being prophetic?

There is no message of hope out of hedonism's aftermath
in this novel for, Nick comments, "We drove on towards
death through the cooling twilight." This was true in the
immediate story but in this novel, death is the end of every-

thing. No reader will read of the Christian message of a journey through the valley of the shadow of death to the glory that will follow. If the shadow of an approaching foe touches anyone, they will not be harmed. Shadows do not hurt and they only come when there is a light. In the valley of the shadow of death, there is, for the believer, a light which is Christ, the Light of the World. This light does not guide anyone in Gatsby's world.

We now learn that while Nick, Tom, Daisy, Gatsby, and Jordan Baker were wilting in the heat of New York, Myrtle Wilson was locked in a room above the garage beside the asheaps. Her husband had locked her in and had told the young Greek Michaelis, who ran the "coffee joint" near the garage, "She's going to stay there till the day after tomorrow and then we're going to move away." When Michaelis returned later to the garage a little after seven, he hears Mrs. Wilson's voice downstairs in the garage. "Beat me," he heard her cry. "Throw me down and beat me, you dirty little coward!" A moment later she rushed out into the dusk and tried to wave down Gatsby's car, "wavered tragically for a moment and then disappeared around the next bend, driven by Daisy." A car going towards New York came to rest a hundred yards beyond. "Its driver hurried back to where Myrtle Wilson, her life violently extinguished, knelt in the road and as her thick dark blood mingled with the dust."

The symbol of the materialism that Myrtle sought, the ostentatious car, kills her. It is called "the death car" in the novel. Other works of literature, of course, lift the theme of the car as the instrument of death. In England, one of the greatest and most popular stories ever written for children is *The Wind in the Willows*. It was written by Kenneth Grahame, a Governor of the Bank of England, and is about the effect of the car in bringing about the death of the countryside as it had been known over many centuries. In days of global warming and damage to the ozone layer pollution is a major international problem. The combustion engine has made a huge contribution to the ravages on the environment. The millions of cars in and around New York and across America today are a huge extension to the car industry of the 1920's. Carnage on the roads and in the environment are rife. Today the United States is, for example, abrogating even the Kyoto Climate Change Treaty for economic reasons.

The death of Myrtle Wilson, where her breast is ripped off, is a potent symbol of where Western Society was going in the 1920's.It is an even more potent symbol as the 21st century rolls in.

In *The Great Gatsby*, then, we see the death of more than just people. In the wake of materialism, there comes, ultimately, the death of the environment for which God gave us custody. In the wake of hedonism comes the death of faithfulness to the marriage bond that God originally set up. It is worth remembering that God set up families long before he ever set up churches. In the novel, we also see the death of women as homemakers. In *The Great Gatsby*, a secure and contented home is unknown. No woman plays her part in building one. The Middle-West, where Nick came from and to where he returns, is always presented as the much more stable place of hearth and home. The potentially nurturing breast of Myrtle Wilson never nourishes.

Tom, Jordan, and Nick eventually come upon the tragedy and the policeman taking his investigative notes. A witness has identified the "death car" as being "yellow" and "new" and going "fifty, sixty." The heartbroken cries of George Wilson show the love he had for his wife. The lying Tom Buchanan, who had told Wilson earlier in the afternoon that the yellow car was his, is now shaking Wilson a little and saying, "That yellow car I was driving this afternoon wasn't mine, do you hear? I haven't seen it all afternoon."

Tom passes close to the table where Myrtle lies, his eyes averting her body, and whispers to Nick, "Let's get out." Myrtle is expendable. Is not lust a heartless beggar? Tom leaves the Wilson's place cursing Gatsby for being a coward in not stopping his car. The fact is that it was his wife who was driving the car at the time of the accident and it was she who was the coward.

In the wake of the death of Myrtle Wilson and Gatsby's dream, Nick finally is sickened at the whole corrupt world he has moved in and out off. He has had his eyes opened and it is a tragic awakening. The legendary glamour of Gatsby's parties is gone and Daisy's legendary voice full of money is now seen for what it is . . . ; it is as money without principle always is, heartless. When, eventually, Nick is invited into the Buchanan household on the evening of Myrtle's death, he refuses the invitation. "I've had enough of all of them for one day," he declares. There is no ambivalence, now. Morally sickened by the whole scene, Nick simply cannot stomach it any longer. He heads down the Buchanan driveway to await the taxi Tom has called for him, only to be confronted by a pink suited Gatsby in the moonlight. Gatsby has promised Daisy that he will keep watch to see if she needs assistance in case Tom causes trouble. The "old sport" phrase is now hollow as Nick learns that Daisy was driving the car at the time of the accident and that Gatsby will cover for her by saying he was at the wheel. The fascination with Gatsby has gone and has now turned to dislike for when Gatsby says that he did not think anybody had seen the accident, Nick says, "I disliked him so much by this time that I didn't find it necessary to tell him he was wrong."

The final scene in chapter seven is of Nick crossing the porch where he had dined with Daisy and Tom "on that June night three months before" to check out on how things were between Tom and Daisy. Nick feared trouble if Tom discovered that Daisy had been driving the car when it killed Myrtle. He looked at the pantry window through a rift between the blind and the sill and found them at the kitchen table with "an unmistakeable air of natural intimacy" and chillingly comments that "anybody would have said they were conspiring together."

Nick leaves Gatsby watching until "Daisy goes to bed" and walks away leaving him standing there in the moonlight, as he puts it, "Watching over nothing."

"Nothing" is a no-nonsense word to describe what *The Great Gatsby* is about. The word "great" in the title is truly ironic. The "greatness" of Gatsby and his dream was, as Shakespeare would have put it, "Much ado about nothing." Death for Gatsby is not very far away, either. The words of Isaiah chapter 40 come as an antidote to Fitzgerald's conclusion about the era he lived through: "All flesh is grass and all its loveliness is like the flower of the field. The grass withers, the flower fades because the breath of the Lord blows upon it; surely the people are grass. The grass withers, the flower fades but the word of our God stands forever . . . even the youths shall faint and be weary and the young men shall utterly fall, but those who wait on the Lord shall renew their strength; they shall mount up with wings like eagles, they shall run and not be weary, they shall walk and not faint." It is best to wait on the Lord any day than to be led by a voice full of money. It is best to wait on the Lord than to wait upon fame, material possessions, or any other earthly dream to deliver what only God can deliver. "Save your life," said the Lord Jesus, "and you will lose it . . . lose your life for my sake and the Gospel's and you will find it." The word "nothing" in this scenario does not feature.

CHAPTER 8

"YOU OUGHT TO HAVE A CHURCH, GEORGE"

Sweet and refreshing sleep was foreign to Nick Carraway the night that followed Myrtle's tragic death. It was foreign to Gatsby, too. Nick, after tossing "half-sick between grotesque reality and savage, frightening dreams," is wakened toward dawn by a taxi going up Gatsby's drive. He decides that he must see Gatsby because he feels he has "something to tell him, something to warn him about." Morning, he feels, would be too late.

Nick finds a very dejected Jay Gatsby. Together they search the enormous house for cigarettes. . . . they are looking for something to dull the ache they are both experiencing. Eventually, after throwing open the french windows of the drawing room, they sit smoking out into the darkness. Nick tries to persuade Gatsby to leave but he is still holding on to some last hope that Daisy might want him back. As they talk, Gatsby opens up his very soul to Nick Carroway about the history of his relationship with Daisy. It is an extraordinary outpouring. First, he spoke of his thrill at being in the world of the rich. Between him and such people, there had always been an "indescribable barbed wire." He spoke of her being the first "nice" girl he had ever known. Her "niceness" seemed to have been tied in with the beautiful house she lived in with a "ripe mystery about it," with its "hint of bedrooms upstairs more beautiful and cool than other bedrooms." Its mystery hinted, he said, at "romances . . . fresh and breathing and redolent of this year's shining motor cars." The link between romance and the motor car has a high priority in Gatsby's life but its link brings death.

The relationship between Gatsby and Daisy became intimate as Gatsby lulls Daisy into "a sense of security. He let her believe that he was a person from much the same strata as himself - that he was fully able to take care of her." Corruption has marked him through his life. His only compass is himself and his dreams. Gatsby then describes to Nick how he genuinely fell in love with Daisy, wooing her all the time with stories of what he was going to do.

War service had sliced into the relationship between Daisy Buchanan and Jay Gatsby and as dawn appeared over Long Island, Gatsby tells Nick what had happened. He had become a major in the army and after the armistice, he had tried "frantically" to get home but "some complication or misunderstanding sent him to Oxford instead." Daisy's letters to him now carried a "quality of nervous despair." She wanted him home, she needed reassurance. The lure of the "artificial" world Daisy lived in began to bring a drift in their relationship. In the evenings, saxophones "wailed" the Beale Street Blues across America "while a hundred pairs of golden and silver slippers shuffled the shining dust." At "the grey tea hour," rooms throbbed with the music of the hour described as a "low sweet fever." There is no moral code to this world. This is a "Jazz Age" which has a serious illness.

Daisy now began to date other men and found that "she wanted her life shaped," but by what force? By love? By money? By practicality? Gatsby was far away and Tom Buchanan was near, so she chose his "bulkiness and position" and by letter to Oxford broke the relationship with Gatsby.

As dawn arrives, Gatsby and Nick begin opening the downstairs windows of Gatsby's mansion. As they do it, Gatsby tries to maintain that Daisy loved him more than she had ever loved Tom. He simply cannot lay his dream to rest.

There follows a discussion of Gatsby's visit to Louisville after his return from Europe. Daisy had gone on her honeymoon. He stayed for a week and revisited the old haunts of his courting days. Daisy's house now had a "melancholy beauty" and as Gatsby left Louisville while sitting in the open vestibule of the day-coach, he watches the town recede and stretches out "his hand desperately as if to snatch only a wisp of air, to save a fragment of the spot that she had made lovely for him."

At nine o'clock, on finishing breakfast, Gatsby and Nick went out on the porch. The gardener informed Gatsby that he wanted to drain the pool later that day because "leaves'll start falling pretty soon" and they would clog up the pipes. Gatsby asks him not "to do it today," telling Nick that he had not used the pool all summer.

Nick eventually tears himself away but not before he tells Gatsby that among a "rotten crowd," he thought Gatsby was worth all of them put together. Nick opines though, in telling his story, that he disapproved of Gatsby "from beginning to end." Yet, there is a juxtaposition in his attitude towards him and alongside his abhorrence of the corruption in Gatsby's life, Nick finds he is moved by his story and by his dream. There is pity in his heart for him and, after all, pity is akin to love. Readers find themselves in a similar position. We abhor the corruption, yet there is something in Gatsby that draws pity in all of us as we see the pathetic wreckage of what chasing an illusion can bring.

Nick finds that he cannot work at his city desk and falls asleep only to be woken at noon by a call from Jordan Baker who wants to see him. He has changed now, though. He has turned against what is going on. He is turning away from the corruption. He is at last taking a moral stand. He is saying, "No!" He has hugely matured overnight. Jordan's voice is now "harsh" and "dry" and leaves him rigid. Their conversation trails off until they "weren't talking any longer." He couldn't remember which one of them hung up the telephone with "a sharp click."

Nick now turns to tell the story of George Wilson in the aftermath of his wife's death and, if any part of the novel presents the question of our accountability to God for our actions, this is it. We learn of Myrtle's sister Catherine arriving "stupid with liquor" at Wilson's place, only to faint and be taken by a "kind and curious" man in his car "in the wake of her sister's body."

People came and went until long after midnight while George "rocked himself back and forth in the couch inside." Eventually he was left alone with Michaelis until dawn. At 3p.m., Wilson began to say that he "had a way of finding out to whom the yellow car belonged." He spoke of his wife having come from the city with her face bruised and her nose swollen. Michaelis, now feeling distinctly uncomfortable, tried to distract Wilson by asking him how long he had been married and if he had any children. He moved uncomfortably around the office and "from time to time" sat down beside Wilson trying "to keep him more quiet."

"Have you got a church you go to sometimes, George?" asks Michaelis. George replies that he does not belong to any. "You ought to have a church, George, for times like this. You must have gone to church once. Didn't you get married in a church? Listen George, listen to me. Didn't you get married in a church?" The only answer Michaelis gets regarding George's connection with a church was that it was "a long time ago." God and the church always lie on the periphery of this novel, there but ignored. Only when death comes is anyone from the church talked about or sought after. These people all live without God. The resulting moral ambivalence, if not chaos, is obvious. Again and again the traumatized George Wilson cries, "Oh, my God!" but he is appealing to the God he has long neglected.

Wilson then draws Michaelis' attention to an expensive dog-leash in a drawer and believes that this is evidence of his wife's infidelity. He also believes that the person with whom she had an affair killed her.

Eventually at dawn, Michaelis turns off the light.One of the moral highpoints of the novel is reached, as Wilson's "glazed eyes turned out to the asheaps." He speaks of how he warned his wife of the living God to whom she must answer. "I spoke to her," he mutters. "I told her she might fool me but she couldn't fool God. I took her to the window . . . and I said . . . God knows what you've been doing, everything you've been doing. You may fool me but you can't fool God."

As Wilson was saying all this, Michaelis noticed "with a shock that he was looking into the eyes of Doctor T.J. Eckleberg which had just emerged, pale and enormous from the dissolving night." "God sees everything," Wilson repeated. To this truth Wilson kept giving his acquiescence by standing with his face close to the window pane, "nodding into the twilight."

There is a phrase often used in Western society today by all kinds of people. Sports personalities use it constantly to speak of the outcome of their commitment to their sport, politicians use it to speak of the outcome of their policies, educationalists use it to speak of the outcome of their work in preparing students for their life work. "After all," they say, with a wistful look, "at the end of the day," this or "at the end of the day," that. This "end of the day" is used to describe some final analysis of what they are about. Where this might be or when is open to a lot of questions.

In George Wilson's view "at the end of the day," we must all answer to God as our final judge. From him nothing will be hidden. It is the biblical view. It was Abraham interceding in prayer for the city of Sodom who cried, "Shall not the judge of all the earth do right?" The Bible's New Testament declares that "God is the judge of all." George Wilson did not believe that the eyes of Dr. T.G. Eckleberg were the eyes of an idol or literally the eyes of God, but he was reminded by them of the fact that God does see everything. The Bible constantly drives this point home. It speaks with certainty of a coming day of universal judgement and states that the Lord Jesus Christ has been appointed the final judge. In the great city of Athens, Paul, the Apostle, declared that "God has appointed a day in which he will judge the world by that man whom he has ordained." To the Roman Christians he wrote, "God shall judge the secrets of men by Jesus Christ according to my Gospel."

The fact that God is a judge is one of His greatest attributes. If God did not care about the difference between right and wrong, then He would not be worthy of worship, would He? The truth of the divine judgement of God is not a bogey, it is a revelation of the moral character of God. It has frightening implications for all those who live godless lives but for those who repent of their sin and trust Christ as their Saviour, it brings meaning to life and dignity to the humblest action. History is not open to the mere whims of men and women. What we do does not end merely by breaking up as Jay Gatsby did like glass against a Tom Buchanan's "hard malice." The Christian view of judgement believes that history is moving towards a goal. It believes that good and God will triumph. It dicards the idea that good and evil will always be in conflict. Evil will, in the final judgement, be finally removed forever. That is a day to relish.

The story of *The Great Gatsby* now moves to the false judgement of George Wilson, who decides not to leave the final judgement of Jay Gatsby to God. He slips away from his garage to Port Roosevelt and then to Gad's Hill at noon. Boys later attested to a man whom they had seen "acting sort of crazy" and also motorists, "at whom he stared oddly from the side of the road." By half-past two, he was in West Egg where he asked the way to Gatsby's house.

Gatsby and his chauffeur, "one of Wolfsheim's protégés," had pumped up a pneumatic mattress and shouldering it, Gatsby had disappeared among the "yellowing trees." He had left a message with his butler that if anyone called, he wanted to be notified. He was waiting for a call from Daisy. Nick states he had an idea that Gatsby himself did not believe it would come "and perhaps no longer cared," commenting, "if that was true he must have felt that he had lost the old warm world and paid a high price for living too long with a single dream."

Afterwards, the butler said he had heard shots but "hadn't thought anything about them." Nick was the first one to raise any alarm when he rushed anxiously up the front steps. He hurried with the chauffeur, the butler, and the gardener down to the pool to find "the laden mattress" moving irregularly down the pool in which could be observed "a thin red circle in the water." Gatsby had been murdered and "a little way off in the grass" lay Wilson's body. "The holocaust," we are told, "was complete."

It is a long journey from the clam-digging, salmon-fishing Jimmy Gatz on the shores of Lake Superior to the dead Jay Gatsby in his summer pool on Long Island. Deception and corruption run through his story and yet, is there not deep grief felt by the reader when it is all over? It is only a story, true, but it is also a parable. It is a parable that warns of the consequences of moral drift, because nobody can break God's moral code and not find that sin has its wages. A person's behaviour is an index of what is in their heart. Gatsby represents all who follow illusive dreams, discarding God's moral code. The consequences are, ultimately, horrendous.

CHAPTER 9

"IT JUST GOES TO SHOW YOU, DON'T IT?"

The general view of Gatsby's death was shaped by someone who bent over Wilson's body on the afternoon of the murder and said, "Madman." The newspapers picked it up the next day in their reports. When Michaelis testified at the inquest and mentioned Wilson's suspicions about his wife, Nick thought the whole story would emerge. Sadly, yet another lie covered it up. Corruption in *The Great Gatsby* is as rife in the last chapter as in every other. It is part of the lives of its characters.

This time the corruption emerges from the tongue of Catherine, Myrtle's sister. She "looked at the coroner with determined eyes under that corrected brow of hers" and "swore that her sister had not been involved with Gatsby," was "completely happy with her husband," and had been in "no mischief whatsoever." She even cried into her handkerchief, "as if the suggestion was more than she could endure." The general public view was, and remained, that Wilson had been a man "deranged by grief." It raises the old question, "Are things ever as they seem?" Fitzgerald shows that even the press in the 1920's was touched by the poisoning of the American dream. Nick observes that the newspaper reports of the murder were "grotesque, circumstantial, eager, and untrue."

In the final chapter of the novel, Fitzgerald subtly uses the funeral of Jay Gatsby to unravel the careless, shallow, irresponsible heart of the "Jazz Age" society. It is an exposure that lingers long in the mind of any serious reader. One wonders just how deeply disenchanted Scott Fitzgerald himself was, with all that went on around him in the end.

Nick Carraway slowly discovers that he is becoming responsible for Gatsby's funeral arrangements. He gives the reason for this by writing that "no one else was interested-interested I mean with that intense personal interest to which everyone has some vague right in the end." In fact Gatsby, in death, hasn't got a friend, if he ever really had one in life, apart from Nick. Nick can hardly believe it when he tries to find people who cared. He states that he found himself "on Gatsby's side and alone."

The first shock is Daisy. Within half an hour of Gatsby's death, Nick "instinctively and without hesitation" telephoned her but no voice "full of money" answers. There is no thrilling response. There is to be no telling him, as she did on the first night he visited her home, how "p-paralyzed with happiness" she was to see him. No more invitations were to come to visit her and no longer would she say, "I love to see you at my table, Nick. You remind me of a - of a rose, an absolute rose." The "stirring warmth" that flowed from Daisy had gone cold with her inability to face up to her responsibilities and to reality. She could not own up to the fact that she had been driving the car that killed Myrtle which had now led to two further deaths. Daisy and Tom had gone away and had left no forwarding address. In these times it would have been called "Daisygate." Here is no honor. Here is no passionate upholding of any moral principle. Maybe Daisy is a 1920's epitome of the godless Darwinian theory of natural selection which removed the need for a moral purpose in natural history. It is the theory that the stronger always eliminates the weaker. The truth of a loving Creator being involved in it all is unnecessary. Myrtle and George Wilson are socially weak. Gatsby, too, is the same. They are all eliminated.

The Bible is very opposed to such a theory, particularly as far as people are concerned. It teaches that God has chosen "the weak things of the world to put to shame the things that are mighty . . . and the things that are not to bring about the things that are"(I Corinthians 1:27-28). In fact the Bible teaches that God's strength is made perfect in weakness. Here is no following of the words of the exhortation of the Bible when it counsels to "Trust in the Lord with all your heart, and lean not on your own understanding; in all your ways acknowledge Him, and He shall direct your paths."

As for Meyer Wolfsheim, Gatsby's partner in corruption, not even he sprang to help. Gatsby's butler was despatched in vain to urge him into "coming out on the next train." The note Wolfsheim sent back with the butler only made things worse. He was "tied up in some very important business" and couldn't get "mixed up in this thing now." He pointed out that he had no information on Gatsby's family "at all."

As Gatsby's circle of acquaintances retreated, Nick answered a telephone call from a man called Slagle who thought he was speaking to Gatsby. The conversation, though vague and sinister, further confirms that Gatsby was not morally blameless in his business connections. Nick, though, honourably carried on helping with the funeral arrangements, proving himself to be a morally responsible person.

The fuller picture of Gatsby and his background is now filled in with the arrival of his father, Henry C. Gatz. He had read of his son's death in a Chicago newspaper. It is a pathetic picture that is drawn for us. Here is "a solemn old man, very helpless and dismayed, bundled up in a long cheap Ulster against the warm September day." His eyes leak continuously. He is shown into the room where his son's body lies and while his grief is genuine, he defines his son, as all the rest of Gatsby's acquaintances have done, by what he owns.

"When he looked around him now for the first time and saw the height and splendour of the hall and the great rooms opening out from it into other rooms, his grief began to be mixed with an awed pride." He speaks of the great future his son had before him and how he didn't want to take his body back to the West, as "Jimmy always liked it better down East." He is sure his Jimmy would have become "a great man" and would have helped "build up the country." The reality, though, was very different.

When the famous "boarder" Klipspringer calls, Nick is appalled to find that he is planning to be at a "sort of picnic or something" with some people he is staying with on the day of the funeral. When pushed by Nick, he weakly says that he will do his best to get away. Nick is disgusted. His disgust turns to rage when Klipspringer says that the reason for his telephone call was because of a pair of tennis shoes he had left at Gatsby's house. He wondered if it wouldn't be too much trouble to have the butler send them to him. Nick hung up the receiver. A pair of tennis shoes mattered more to Klipspringer than Gatsby and all the hospitality he had ever shown him did. What were the words to the song he played on the night Gatsby showed Daisy his mansion? "In the morning and in the evening, ain't we got fun." Fun, that's it, fun. He lived for fun and could not care less about the people who he thought could provide him with it. How insubstantial Klipspringer's kind of fun is! It plays tennis and goes to picnics in the face of death and eternity and does not want to know about either.

On the morning of the funeral, Nick Carraway goes to New York to try to reach Meyer Wolfsheim. This is the Wolfsheim who once praised Gatsby to Nick as a "fine fellow . . . handsome to look at and a perfect gentleman . . . the kind of man you'd like to take home and introduce to your mother and sister." He wasn't leaving his "home" for Gatsby's funeral, that was for certain.

Nick had to push open Wolfsheim's door and was faced with his secretary, Stella. She protests strongly that her boss, heard whistling tunelessly behind a partition, is in Chicago. Lies and deceit continue to be common currency even on the morning of Gatsby's funeral. On hearing Nick mention Gatsby's name, circumstances suddenly change and Stella vanishes to inform Wolfsheim that Nick has arrived. Wolfsheim now appears in the doorway "holding out both hands." He even talks, we are told, "in a reverent voice" saying that "it was a sad time for us all." All he has to offer is a cigar.

Wolsheim speaks of how he "made Gatsby," first finding him as a hard up major fresh from World War I, without regular clothes and hungry. He boasts of raising Gatsby "out of nothing." Why, they were always together in everything. Nick immediately points out that since Wolfsheim was Gatsby's closest friend, he knows Wolfsheim will want to come to Gatsby's funeral that afternoon. Pathetic crocodile tears follow and a pleading that when a man gets killed, he must not get "mixed up in it." As a younger man, he says he would have stayed with a friend to the bitter end but now he only shows friendship for a man when he is alive. Now he has a "rule" that after the death of a friend, he will "let everything alone." Even the ungodly have rules and maxims, but this ungodly Jew does not follow the teachings of his forefathers to whom God gave the Ten Commandments on Mt. Sinai. He does not even follow the Levitical injunction to "love your neighbour as yourself" (Leviticus 19:18). Here self-centeredness and self-protection is epitomized. Machiavelli's teachings still lived and were being followed by Wolfsheim. People were things to be manipulated. Good character was obsolete and foolish. The wolf "who fixed the World Series in 1919" shrinks off the pages of this novel, not only having poisoned the American sport but also having poisoned the very meaning of friendship. The very sky has turned dark and Nick goes back to bury Gatsby in a drizzle.

There is no relenting of the exposure of the mind and morals of the "Jazz Age" as the novel comes to its conclusion. The demands of virtue find no takers in this crowd. Nick comes in from the drizzle and after changing his clothes, he finds Henry Gatz full of excitement walking up and down in the hall of his son's mansion, asking him to look at a photograph, "cracked in the corners and dirty with many hands." It was a picture of Gatsby's mansion that he had sent his father. The point is that it was the mansion to which Mr. Gatz was clinging to as evidence of true greatness. Gatsby had bought his father a house two years before. Even the farmer from Minnesota is poisoned with materialistic thinking and blinded to how his son's money was made.

Mr. Gatz produced an old copy of a book called *Hopalong Cassidy* which his son had owned as a child. In it is evidence of his childhood habits of seeking to improve himself. It lists a schedule of rising at 6 a.m. followed by exercising, studying, work, sports, education, and "poise and how to attain it." There is a list of general resolves including "No wasting time at Shafters" no more "smoking and chewing," and of reading "one improving book or magazine per week." "It just goes to show you don't it?" says Gatz. Henry Gatz had an American dream too: hard work and self improvement leads to financial success and material gain. Anything was possible for "Jimmy." Gatz had not followed the dream himself but his son had. Sadly, the spiritual is left out of Jimmy

Gatz's childhood list. The whole idea of dying to self and living for God and the good of others is anathema in this dream. For Henry Gatz, his son was one of those people who was "born to succeed." What he did not know was that the corruption at the root of his ways and practices made him ultimately "born to fail."

Now the hour of three o'clock in the afternoon strikes and the Lutheran minister from the denomination whose college Gatsby had so despised arrives to lead the funeral proceedings. The great mansion is virtually empty of people. No Chester Beckers, now. The Leeches are nowhere to be seen. Bunsen's flame is burning somewhere else. Dr. Civet is dead. The Willie Voltaires stand around no more and the Blackbucks no longer gather in a corner. The Ismays and the Ripley Snells do not come. No Da Fontano promotes sympathy and Klipspringer plays no dirge. Benny McClenahan does not arrive with any girl. Mr. Jewett, once head of the American Legion, does not even come to pay his last respects to the once decorated army major. The Duke, "the prince of something," is not princely in showing sympathy for he shows none. The whole party-going entourage is nowhere to be seen.

The Lutheran minister glances at his watch and wonders when the proceedings are to begin. Nick takes him aside and asks him to wait for half an hour. The truth is it would not matter how long they waited because it would not be of any use. The party goers are not interested when the party is over. When the buffet tables with their "garnished hors- d'oeuvre's, spiced hams crowded against salads of harlequin designs, and pastry pigs and turkeys bewitched to a dark gold" are no longer spread out on tables under canvas on Gatsby's lawn, the feasting crowds don't want to know Gatsby, dead or alive. When the bar in the main hall of Gatsby's mansion is no longer set up with its stock of gins, liquors, and cordials, the hundreds who drank from it would not even take an afternoon off to pay their last respects by standing in the hall as Gatsby's body is taken for burial.

These people are an echo of the crowd who wanted to make Christ King on His feeding of the five thousand. He would have none of it. His kingdom was not to be based on people's love of a free meal but who had absolutely no personal interest in the one who provided it. In *The Great Gatsby*, people take from a corrupt hand and ignore the hand. In real life, millions of people take from God's bounty every day as He spreads their tables with good things, but they have no interest whatsoever in God. In the Lord's Prayer, we are called to reverence God's name even before we ask for our daily bread. To reverence God's name is more important than anything else in our lives. In doing it, everything else we do is influenced. It even gives our daily bread significance.

What, then, are Nick Carraway's thoughts as he stands by the graveside of Jay Gatsby? He tells us that he tried to think of Gatsby for a moment but that "he was already too far away" and that he could "only remember, without resentment, that Daisy hadn't sent a message or a flower." Maybe Nick feels sorry for Daisy as the victim of Tom Buchanan's cruelty and Jay Gatsby's dream. While it could be argued that Daisy is, in part, a victim, this does not let her off the hook. Hers is heartless behavior. She has a huge dearth of compassion and is guilty of downright moral irresponsibility.

As his story slowly ends, Nick returns in heart, mind, soul, and body to the Middle West. It is a Middle West he particularly remembers returning to at Christmas during his college days. Here is hearth, home, and snow, "real snow, our snow." Here are "the street lamps and sleigh bells in the frosty dark and the shadows of holly wreaths thrown by lighted windows on the snow." Here are dwellings that are "still called through the decades by a family name." *The Great Gatsby* is "a story of the West after all - Tom, Gatsby, Daisy, Jordan, and I were all Westerners and perhaps we possessed some deficiency in common that made us subtly unadaptable to Eastern life." Nick's view of the East is now forever distorted even in his dreams and is incorrectable. When autumn comes, he goes back home. His view of life finally becomes one where he concludes that "life is more successfully looked at from a single window after all." This view avoids like a plague many of the complexities of life and experience and though it is truly understandable, it is not intellectually or morally healthy.

Before Nick goes home, he decides to visit Jordan Baker. He wanted, he says, "to leave things in order." This is something that life consistently refuses to do. He has already said at the beginning of his story that when he returned home, he "wanted the world to be in uniform." The meeting with Jordan turns out to be a strangely nasty, even bitter meeting. Jordan tells him that she is engaged to someone else. Nick feigns surprise but secretly doubts the ever - deceiving Jordan. He is, though, still "half in love" with her . Wondering if he was making a mistake, he quickly decides to finally finish the relationship. Jordan, though, makes one final summary of what she thinks of him. She reminds him that he once said "a bad driver was only safe until she met another bad driver." She tells him that he is that other bad driver and that he is guilty of being a secretly proud person. It is a cruel metaphor to use, especially in the light of Daisy's irresponsible driving. Life does not tie up relationships in any "uniform" and this relationship ends, sadly and coldly.

The wooden, passionless conversation between Jordan and Nick now gives place to Nick's last meeting with Tom Buchanan. He sees him walking as aggresively as ever on Fifth Avenue in New York, "his hands out a little from his body as if to fight off interference." Nick does not want to interfere but Tom sees him and walks back towards him, holding out his hand. Nick refuses to shake it and forces Tom into admitting

that he told George Wilson on the afternoon of the murder
that Jay Gatsby was the owner of the car that killed Myrtle. He
still believed that Gatsby had been the driver. Daisy had still
kept her sordid secret. Tom's conclusion was that Gatsby
deserved death. "He had it coming to him," he snarls. As Tom
disappears into a jewelry store, Nick comments that he was
"rid of my provincial squeamishness for ever."

Here we have a fascinating place in the novel. Nick's Midwestern capacity to be easily shocked and overscrupulous
about moral responsibility is contrasted with Tom's capacity to
overcome his own provincial background and ability and with
Daisy's to "smash up things and creatures" and then to return to
"their money or their vast carelessness, or whatever it was that
kept them together, and let other people clean up the mess they
had made . . . " Daisy and Tom escape immediate judgment for
their actions. Tom Buchanan, particularly, epitomizes the
famous words of the psalmist, Asaph, in Psalm 73 when he
wrote of observing the prosperity of the wicked. "There are no
pangs in their death," he wrote, "but their strength is firm. They
are not in trouble as other men, nor are they plagued like other
men. Therefore pride serves as their necklace; violence covers
them as a garment. Their eyes bulge with abundance; they have
more than heart could wish. . . . and they say, 'How does God
know? And is there knowledge in the Most High?' Behold, these
are the ungodly who are always at ease; they increase in riches."

The psalmist nearly loses his foothold because of the
phenomenon of the seemingly unjudged wicked, but he eventually comes to realize that they will one day have to face God
in judgment and experience His punishment. They are closer
to Hell than they can ever imagine. Asaph then berates himself for unspiritual thinking and soars in his faith when he
realizes that God will guide him with His counsel and will, as
he puts it, "Afterward receive me to glory." He adds, "Whom
have I in heaven but You? And there is none upon earth that I

desire besides You. My flesh and my heart fail: but God is the strength of my heart and my portion forever." It is true that if there is not a final judgment then Heaven will turn black. Heaven, for sure, will never turn black.

So Nick comes to his last night in West Egg. He goes over to look at "the huge incoherent failure of a house once more." Some boy with a piece of brick had scrawled an obscene word on the front steps, now highlighted by the moonlight. Even the children of the area experienced corruption. Nick could not bear it and erased the word with his shoe. He does not want to remember the place of Gatsby's dreams by an obscene word.

It is a fact that more critical writing exists on *The Great Gatsby* than on any other work of American fiction. This is not surprising, for here we are dealing with the very nature of our souls. The ending of the novel, in particular, makes an attempt to sum up the nature of chasing dreams. Here we find Nick deep into soul searching. The last few lines are reckoned to be among the very greatest of American fiction.

Nick went down to the beach and "sprawled out on the sand" as the moon rose higher. Suddenly, he began to think of the dream that first met the Dutch sailors who immigrated there as they gazed on that "fresh, green breast of the new world." The American dream he felt was "the last and greatest of all human dreams. For a transitory enchanted moment, man must have held his breath in the presence of this continent, compelled into an aesthetic contemplation he neither understood nor desired, face to face for the last time in history with something to commensurate his capacity for wonder."

Nick sat on that shore brooding even further on "the old world." It was not a careless brooding. "Dwell on the past," says the Russian proverb "and you will lose an eye. Ignore the past and you will lose both of them." Somehow, though, that first American dream of the Dutch sailors is linked in Nick's

mind with Jay Gatsby's dream. He thought of the green light of
Daisy's dock and of the dream Gatsby had for recreating the
romance he had in the past. It was, of course, a hopeful, hope-
less dream; because what Gatsby did not realize was that "it
was already behind him, somewhere back in that vast obscurity beyond the city, where the dark fields of the republic rolled
on under the night." His conclusion is that "the green light, the
orgastic future," will never be ours. We hope it will. Our hope
of it keeps us going but "we beat on, boats against the current,
borne back ceaselessly into the past." That autumnal evening
on that Long Island beach was very Keatsian, almost as hope-
less as having one's name written on water.

CHAPTER 10

"ONE FINE MORNING"

~ A personal response to *The Great Gatsby* ~

My interest in F. Scott Fitzgerald has always been deeply influenced by a book written by the literary agent and former actress, Katinka Matson. Entitled "Short Lives"(Picador by Pan Books Ltd, 1981), the book contains "portraits of writers, painters, poets, actors, musicians, and performers in pursuit of death." All of the people written about were highly creative people whose very creativity seemed to embody the pursuit of self-destruction and death. Malcolm Lowry called them "the burnt out ones."

In Matson's "Short Lives" are the stories of people like Janis Joplin, Jack London, Marilyn Monroe, Sylvia Plath, Elvis Presley, Dylan Thomas, Vincent van Gogh, Simone Weil, Judy Garland, and James Dean. Matson also includes the story of F. Scott Fitzgerald and she has indelibly captured for me the sense of the tragic in his life.

There is no question that for many people, Scott and Zelda Fitzgerald epitomized the decade of the 1920's. They

were married in New York City in March 1920 and honey-
mooned in the Biltmore Hotel. They snacked on champagne
and fresh spinach, cart wheeled down the halls, and dove into
the fountain at the Plaza until their outrageous behaviour led
to their expulsion. The rest of Scott Fitzgerald's story is a
poignant tale of a writing genius made sick by drinking and
excessive living. Zelda was eventually diagnosed as a schizo-
phrenic and hospitalized. Fitzgerald died on December 21,
1940, of a cardiac spasm while reading the *"Princeton Alumni
Weekly."* He was forty-four years old. His wife Zelda died tragically in a fire at Highlands Hospital in Asheville, North Carolina eight years later.

It is easy to dismiss Fitzgerald as a hard-drinking playboy
but his writing stands as a barrier to such stereotyping. There
is no way I want to respond to the man who wrote *The Great
Gatsby* with a shrug. His work is a classic by any standard,
meticulously crafted and, in many ways, beautifully written.
The themes of the novel are wide ranging. Here is aspiration in
an American setting. Here is romanticism, seeing, judging,
love, wealth, and history. Here is the theme of time. There are,
in fact, 450 time words in the novel (A.T.Crosland Concor-
dance to *The Great Gatsby*: Detroit: Gale research, 1975). The
work deals with the theme of modern communication of ideas
through newspapers, movies, and theaters. The imagery and
symbolism in the novel include the use of color, cars, flowers,
light and darkness, weather, landscape, and eyes. Here is the
loss of moral certainties and public obligations. Here love
meets money and adultery meets class. Illusion and reality also
meet violently, and the dead hand of the past and the high
intensions of the future clash. Fitzgerald also deals with con-
sumerism, Prohibition, and organized crime. The juxtaposi-
tions of beauty and squalor, peace and violence, vitality and
decay are everywhere, and Fitzgerald does all of this in nine
short chapters of a novel!

For me, though, the novel has always been a useful warning. I am well aware that Fitzgerald was not trying to preach the Gospel of Jesus Christ in his novel nor in his life. Yet as Dr. Kate Maurer states, though Fitzgerald "is not espousing a heavy-handed Christian message," he is "encouraging readers to stop and take inventory of their lives" and is "urging a reconsideration of where society is and where it is going" (Cliffs Notes, IDG Books Worldwide, Inc.). The eyes of Dr. T. J. Eckleberg haunt the novel and Gatsby's world is one where value systems are far removed from the Ten Commandments. The novel is a warning that the lifestyle of the 1920's "Jazz Age" generation was not all the joy and pleasure it seemed to be. It is a parable of the frightening dangers of moral ambiguity and drift.

It has been pointed out that the market place of *The Great Gatsby* is located on Broadway and the geography of the story encircles it. Wolfshiem operates there. Nick and Jordan begin their courtship there. Gatsby breaks up with Daisy there. Daisy, we are told, is appalled by West Egg, "this unprecedented 'place' that Broadway had begotten upon a Long Island fishing village." This Broadway ethos certainly leads to destruction in the novel. Somehow even the modern day Mark Twain, Garrison Keillor, fits much better at home in Minnesota than he does on Broadway. There are shades of Nick Caraway and his love for the Middle-West in Keillor's life.

Fitzgerald's style of writing has affected all of his readers. His use of metaphor and simile, his visual images, and his concise exactness are enchanting and, at times, deeply perturbing as well as being apt. He was a serious writer, despite his lifestyle, and it was his stated aim to make what he had to say and the way of saying it indissoluble. *The Great Gatsby* is a great American novel but it is also more. It is the universality of its themes that makes it a novel that challenges us all, wherever we may live, to think deeply about what life and values are all about. The novel has a long shadow that touches millions who live far from Long Island in the summer of 1922.

A lot of critics have taken the road to East and West Egg. They include T.S. Elliot, Edith Wharton, Gertrude Stein, F.R. Leavis, H.L. Menecken, and L.P. Hartley to name but a few. Comments across the last seven decades have continued to appear and fresh insight might yet come relating *The Great Gatsby* to themes like gender, feminism, and post-modernism.

My deepest reaction to the novel, though, has to do with its ultimate message of hopelessness. As it happens, before I was born, my mother lived in the United States during the 1920's before she came home to settle in Northern Ireland for the rest of her life. She too had emigrated to "that green breast of the world" but the "green breast of Ireland" eventually caught her (See "The Hawthorn Scent," Ambassador-Emerald). I know her story better now since reading *The Great Gatsby* and understand why she so deeply rejected the moral stance of much of the 1920's generation around her.

One day she came into my room when I was a teenager and it was obvious that something had truly excited her. She had a Bible in her hand and had been reading the Bible story of Mary and Martha's reaction when Christ had visited their home at Bethany. In the story, Martha kept busy but Mary sat at Christ's feet and heard His word. Her sister berated her but Jesus answered, "Martha, Martha, you are worried about many things but one thing is needed, and Mary has chosen that good part which will not be taken away from her." My mother looked at me with deep insight and said, "What Mary learned that day of Christ was never taken away from her - not in time nor eternity! What you learn of Christ you take with you!"

Nick Carraway muses as he lies on the beach at East Egg before he heads home on the "orgastic future that year by year recedes before us." Fitzgerald, we know, deliberately chose the word "orgastic." Ultimately, though, the view is taken that no matter what we go after in life, we are all borne ceaselessly into the past. He is saying that after death, there is nothing. We are merely history.

The Christian view is the very opposite. What Mary learned from Christ was that beyond death, there is resurrection. Out of all of Christ's followers, she was the only one who believed in His resurrection. His disciples did not. Joseph and Nicodemus brought spices to Christ's tomb and left them there to take away the stench of death. They were not expecting His resurrection. Even Mary Magdalene was not expecting to see Christ alive again because she said to the man that she thought was the gardener, "Sir, if you have carried Him away, tell me where you have laid Him and I will take Him away." But Christ's body was not to see corruption (See Psalm 10:10 and Acts 2:27). Mary of Bethany, knowing this, poured out very costly oil of spikenard on His feet at her home. When Judas spoke out against it, saying the spikenard could have been given to the poor, Christ said, "Let her alone: she has kept this for the day of my burial." In other words, because Mary believed Christ's word she knew He would not need the spikenard in death so she gave it to Him in life! This message is at the very heart of the Christian message. "If Christ is not risen," Paul said, "your faith is futile." The apostles took the resurrection message to the world and asserted that because Christ lives, "we shall live also." Life in Christ is not a rowing against the tide borne ceaselessly into the past. It is moving forward towards a future that will be not merely "orgastic" but permanently blissful. It was as a prisoner of the Romans that Paul wrote some incredible words. Despite experiencing huge desertion from many people and knowing loneliness, cold, and the fear of possible execution, does he speak of being borne hopelessly into the past? Certainly not. He says, "Finally there is laid up for me a crown of righteousness, which the Lord, the righteous judge, will give to me on that day: and not to me only, but to all who have loved His appearing" (2 Timothy 4:8).

John the apostle, in exile on the island of Patmos for his faith, wrote that he was given a vision of "a new heaven and a new earth and saw the holy city, New Jerusalem." There, he says, "God shall wipe away every tear from their eyes: there shall be no more death, nor sorrow, nor crying. There shall be no more pain, for the former things have passed away. . . ." There he saw no temple, "for the Lord God Almighty and the Lamb are its temple. The city had no need for the sun or moon to shine in it, for the glory of God illuminated it. The Lamb is its light; and the nations of those who are saved shall walk in it and the kings of the earth shall bring their glory and honour into it . . . its gates shall not be shut at all by day . . . and they shall bring the glory and honour of nations into it. There shall by no means enter into it anything that defiles or causes abomination or a lie, but only those who are written in the Lamb's Book of Life . . .There shall be no night there . . . and they shall reign forever and ever" (Revelation 21:2-5, 22-27; 22:5). It is, said Jesus, a place of "many mansions." There is no mansion like Gatsby's that is "one great incoherent failure." No child on any step scrawls an obscene word.

I appreciate the genius of F. Scott Fitzgerald. I appreciate his honesty and the unforgettable way he captured the emptiness of hedonism and the ultimate cruelty of materialism. I am deeply aware of the awesome way he depicts a youthful dream, captivating a life to the exclusion of reality. He certainly proves that we cannot repeat our past. Yet, I sincerely believe that the conclusion of the novel is wrong. Death is not the end. The words of John 3:16 belie such a belief: "For God so loved the world, that he gave his only begotten Son, that whoever believes in him should not perish, but have everlasting life." At the beginning of a new millennium, Christ is the hope of the world. Those who repent toward God and put their faith and trust in Christ as Saviour can know a hope beyond the grave that ends in indescribable glory. One fine morning, indeed.

BIBLIOGRAPHY

"A Life In Letters": F. Scott Fitzgerald. A new collection edited and annotated by Matthew J. Bruccoli. A Touchstone Book. Published by Simon and Schuster Inc. 1995.

"F. Scott Fitzgerald: *The Great Gatsby*: Essays, articles, reviews." Edited by Nicolas Tredell. Columbia Critical Guides. Columbia University Press.1999.

"The American Novel": New essays on *The Great Gatsby*. Edited by Matthew J. Bruccoli. Cambridge University Press 1985.

"Short Lives" by Katinka Matson. Picador by Pan Books Ltd. 1981.

The Great Gatsby: An introduction. Gillian Traub. Private research.

Fitzgerald's *The Great Gatsby* by Kate Maurer, Ph.D. CliffsNotes. IDG Books Worldwide, Inc.

The Great Gatsby, F. Scott Fitzgerald. Notes by Dr. Julian Cowley. York Notes Advanced. Longman / York Press.

The Holy Bible, New King James Version. Copyright by Thomas Nelson, Inc.1982

The Great Gatsby, Paramount, 1974
   Screenwriter: Francis Ford Coppola (based on the novel).
   Cast: Robert Redford (Jay Gatsby); Mia Farrow (Daisy Buchanan); Bruce Dern (Tom Buchanan); Sam Waterson (Nick Carraway); Lois Chiles (Jordan Baker); Karen Black (Myrtle Wilson); Scott Wilson (George Wilson); Edward Hermann(Klipsringer); Howard da Silva (Meyer Wolfsheim); Roberts Blossom (Mr. Gatz) Running Time:145 minutes.

"God's Funeral" by A.N. Wilson . Abacus 2000.

Other Books Authored by Derick Bingham
Published by Ambassador-Emerald

THE HAWTHORN SCENT
*Of an Irish Springtime
and a spiritual journey*

An Autobiography in Verse

In this unique autobiography-in-verse the author traces his journey from childhood by the beautiful Mountains of Mourne through his school and University days to adult life. He writes of the challenge of a call to the Christian ministry worldwide and of serving through years of terrorism and civil strife. Here is a kaleidoscope of people who have crossed the author's path and experiences that have shaped his life. It is an autobiography that is wistful, sometimes exhilarating, sometimes sad, often humorous but always filled with hope.

In his introduction the author states, "Life is filled with touches. The sweetness of a long kiss backed by fidelity. The power of a story well told. The searing wound of sarcasm. The bewildering influence of a cold shoulder. The enlightenment of a good teacher. The fickleness of hype. The sound of the cataracts of death around the bend. The clutch of a little baby's hand on an adult's small finger. The shadows cast by moonlight. The greeting of the rising sun. The sound of rain driving against a bedroom window. The inspiration of a great orchestra. We are all touched by something. Here then are some of the things that have touched my life on my spiritual journey. I trust that what is good will touch you, too. It all began in an Irish Springtime. . . ."

A wonderfully written and beautifully illustrated hardback book. Illustrations by *Ross Wilson.

*Ross Wilson is a famous artist and sculptor. His work can be found in places as diverse as the James Joyce Museum, Dublin, The National Portrait Gallery, London and Harvard University, Cambridge, USA.

Hardback $19.99/£12.99

DIARY OF A LONGING HEART
A 365 Day Journey Through the Life of David

Takes the reader on a daily walk through the eventful life of David. This 365-day devotional traces David's life from unknown shepherd boy to famous king. When David wrote, he expressed the universal heart of man as he relates to his Creator.

Paperback $9.99/£5.95

FOR ALL SEASONS
Daily Devotions for Folk in the Fast Lane!

This devotional book is designed to be an oasis of calm to those people in life's fast lane. God's Word has truth for every season of life, trust Him and that pounding heart will beat more gently; that ashen face will begin to fill with color and God, who is always faithful, will reveal His love.

Paperback $11.99/£7.99

ON HIGHEST GROUND
Surveying Your Resources in Christ

Ephesians gives one of the most magnificent views in Scripture of a Christian's resources in Christ. This book goes through this exquisite letter verse by verse in a daily reading form. Here is salvation by grace. Here is a description of what true Christian unity is all about. Here too is redemption through Christ's blood, forgiveness of sins, adoption into God's family, sealing by the Holy Spirit and incomparable power for living, the very same power that raised Christ from the dead.

Paperback $15.99/£9.99

THE INVITATION
365 Devotions from John's Gospel

Daily readings to provide insight into the Gospel of John. John was written to give early believers a fuller knowledge of Christ and Christianity. This book examines, among others, Peter the Impulsive, Thomas the Cautious, Pilate the Worldly and Andrew the Missionary.

Paperback $12.99/£7.99

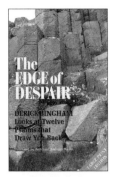

THE EDGE OF DESPAIR
Looks at Twelve Psalms that Draw You Back

The study of twelve Psalms shows a way of escape from despair to the heights of God's grace. Read how David's cries of despair always ended in rejoicing in God's goodness.

Paperback $6.99/£3.50

WALKING WITH GOD
*For those who have lost their way
and are uncertain where to turn*

This book seeks to give answers to questions frequently asked by Christians on guidance, backsliding, worry, suffering and values. It allows us to see who we are, what direction we are taking, and where our destination will be. For those who have grown cold in heart, weary in spirit, bitter of temperament and now follow the Lord at a distance, Derick Bingham brings a Biblical perspective showing us how to fulfil the purpose God has for us.

This is the 'Pathway Series' all in one book!

Paperback $9.99/£5.99

WHEN THE STORKS FLEW SOUTH
Decisions That Changed History

This book examines how history has been deeply influenced by the decisions people make. Abraham Lincoln at Gettysburg changed the face of a nation; Napoleon marched on Moscow in winter and had his army virtually frozen to death; the "unsinkable" Titanic was lost because the outlooks were not given binoculars. The book ends with Pilot's decision to capitulate to the Jews.

Paperback $8.99/£4.99